LIONS
KING OF BEASTS

Lee Server

TODTRI

This edition produced exclusively for W.H. Smith Limited by
Todtri Productions Limited
P.O. Box 20058
New York, NY 10023–1482

Printed and Bound in Singapore

ISBN 1–880908–08–5

Author: Lee Server

Producer: Robert M. Tod
Book Designer: Mark Weinberg
Editor: Mary Forsell
Photo Editor: Natasha Milne
Design Associate: Jackie Skroczky

TABLE OF CONTENTS

INTRODUCTION

The majestic lion is the legendary ruler of the animal kingdom. Revered for its strength and bravery, the lion has been a symbol of supremacy since the beginning of recorded history.

How did the lion ascend to the throne in a kingdom full of fierce contenders? It is not the largest of animals. Measured in full length, the average male lion is no larger than 10 feet (3.1 metres) from nose to tail. It is not the strongest of animals, nor the fastest. Its skills as a hunter are, in fact, deeply flawed. With its plain brown or sandy body colouration and tufted tail, the lion also does not by any means possess the most beautiful coat nor rival the plumage of other animals in its habitat.

And yet its position remains nearly uncontested. Certainly, there are few human observers who have seen a full-grown lion in the wild who would ever question its supremacy. It has much to do with bearing. The lion conveys grandeur and self-assurance. This is particularly true of a grown male, which possesses a magnificent mane, so much like a king's ceremonial headdress or an Indian chief's war bonnet. There is the undoubted fierceness of the lion in battle and in destroying its prey. And there is that roar, a low grumble building in intensity, used to signify territoriality and power. The lion has learned how to make this roar send a vibrating signal throughout its domain, literally making the earth quake. And then, equally impressive, is the lion's catlike aura of intelligence, conveying a sense of subtle thought processes at work. For such things and more does the lion justly claim its crown.

The lion has long been a symbol of superiority. The lion's body is the basis for the Egyptian sphinx, which has the head of a human, ram, or hawk. Usually representing courage and domination, the lion is a symbolic motif in the Bible and also appears in many folk tales, including Aesop's fables. Throughout this century, the lion's image has appeared frequently, associated with every-

thing from sports teams to men's clubs to insurance companies. Even the movie industry has employed the lion's image: Beginning in the 1920s, Leo the Lion became the impressive corporate symbol for Metro-Goldwyn-Mayer, the Hollywood studio.

Despite the lion's exalted status, man has made this animal's continued existence a problem in some cases and an impossibility in others. Various lion subspecies once roamed across large stretches of Europe and Asia. But the growing hordes of humankind, with their need to expand their domain and to tame the wilderness, successfully chased several lion subspecies right into extinction. In other cases, vast lion populations were reduced—through hunting, habitat loss, and other factors—to a small, lonely enclave. Were it not for the efforts in this century of a tiny number of prescient and dedicated conservationists, both professional and amateur, even more damage might have been done.

As of this writing, the lion is not an officially labelled "endangered species." African governments have made great improvements in maintaining national parks and sanctuaries and in protecting the animals residing there from hunters and poachers. The old days of massive lion-hunting safaris, when mostly visiting amateur "sportsmen" wounded or killed countless thousands of lions, are no more.

Lions in captivity now thrive and breed freely in their unusual surroundings. Furthermore, scientific research into the genetics of particular lion subspecies may eventually help to increase the number of lions in the wild by introducing captive-raised lions to that environment. And in India, naturalists continue to work to increase that continent's one and only remaining population of Asiatic lions, hoping to successfully introduce the subspecies beyond their current single, small enclave in the Gir National Park and Lion Sanctuary.

But in a world where wilderness habitat is lost to the tractor every minute of every day, where governments feel they must put their ambitions and their expanding human population's needs ahead of a wild animal's right to exist, and where numerous species come close to extinction each year, it would be naive to believe the lion's future is entirely certain. Various organizations in Africa, the United States, and around the world must work throughout the year just to prevent the world's lion population from losing any more ground.

In the following pages, we will explore the

origins of these magnificent monarchs of the wild, as well as the colourful family tree of all the cats, determining how much the fierce lion has in common with its cousin the common, domesticated feline. We will examine the distinctive nature of lions—their methods of hunting, mating, and raising cubs. Lions are the only sociable cat, living not alone or in pairs like other cats, but in large, familial groups called "prides". Examining the pride's intricate social hierarchy, we will see that life for a lion family member can involve both selfish brutality and great kindness and generosity.

The text will also chart the sometimes inspiring but too often violent and destructive relationship between lion and man. Demonising the lion as a man-eating monster allowed for the senseless "sporting" slaughter of whole lion prides. But in one case, at least, recalled in detail herein—the story of Elsa the Lioness, and Joy and George Adamson—the relationship between lion and man proved to be constructive and mutually respectful.

In our tour of lion country, we will also examine the various animal reserves where lions can be viewed in the wild and learn of the field and lab work being done to ensure that the lion's future will be a bright one.

THE HISTORY OF THE LION

Lions are members of the cat family, whose original ancestors date back some twelve million years. The various types of cats have actually changed very little in all of that time.

The proper family name for cats is Felidae. Under this family heading are three genera, or groupings, of cats: *Panthera*, *Acinonyx*, and *Felis*. The fast-moving cheetah, native to Africa and large parts of eastern and southern Asia, is the only member of the *Acinonyx* group. The *Felis* group includes all the smaller cats, both wild and domestic, from *F. concolor* (the fierce American puma or mountain lion) to *F. catus* (the common domestic cat). The remaining cats all belong to the *Panthera* genus. These include the big cats of legend, the roaring royalty of the jungle, forest, and savannah: the leopard (*P. pardus*) and its variants, the snow leopard (*P. uncia*) and clouded leopard (*P. nebulosa*); the tiger (*P. tigris*); and, of course, wildlife's uncontested king, the lion (*P. leo*).

Despite their very different worlds and ways of living, the various groups of cats remain close cousins in a variety of ways. Unlikely as it would first seem, the untamed African lion has much in common with the pampered pussycat curled up in a suburban living room. Those observing lions in the wild are often struck by how frequently the huge and dangerous animals re-create the poses and personality traits of a pet tabby. Similarly, the housecat, domesticated only a mere four thousand years ago (a fraction of the time that the dog has been domesticated), has retained hunting instincts and other feral abilities that link it to the regal lion.

As for the lion, natural scientists are only now just beginning to understand the capacity for diversity and adaptation of which the King of Beasts is capable.

FROM PREHISTORIC TIMES TO THE PRESENT

It was only in recent times that lions became known as animals of Africa. In bygone centuries, they could be found even more widely throughout Africa and in many other lands, including Europe and Asia. A species known as the cave lion lived in Europe during the late Ice Age. Profiles of lions were etched into the walls of caves in France more than fifteen thousand years ago.

Since the advent of recorded history, the lion has not existed in the wild anywhere in Europe, with the exception of Greece. Lions were reported as common in that country in 500 B.C., but by 300 B.C., Aristotle described them as being rare, and by A.D. 100, there were no further recorded sightings of lions in Greece. They did continue to exist in Palestine for many more centuries, finally disappearing from that region at the time of the Crusades.

To understand the history of the lion, it is necessary to understand the conditions that it needs to exist. Despite its reputation as the King of the Jungle, the lion actually does not inhabit jungles, nor does it live in very dry deserts or in the rain forests. Instead, the lion exists in what is termed scrub country.

It lives in some areas that have intense heat, but it also exists in some locales with cool climates. In fact, lion tracks have been found on Mount Kenya at altitudes of more than 2 miles (3.2 kilometres). But in most cases, it lives among grassy plains and thorny scrub trees. Historically, as the areas it inhabits have lost these characteristics, the lion has departed or has been driven out.

The lion's exit from Europe in prehistoric times was most likely the result of the massive spreading of forests throughout the continent, making the area uninhabitable for this animal. In the more recent past, we can clearly survey the

shrinking distribution of the world's lion population, its total disappearance from areas it once called home in India, the Middle East (including Iran and northern Africa), and in parts of southern Africa. In all of these cases, mankind was directly responsible for the elimination of the lions or of the lions' habitat. As populations increased in the above areas, wilderness became towns and farmland, eliminating open grass and scrub. And as the lion lost its habitat to the plow, it increasingly lost its life to human weaponry. By the time of the invention of the high-powered hunting rifle, the lion had basically lost any chance of maintaining its homeland.

VANISHED SUBSPECIES

The vanished subspecies include the Cape lion, which roamed through southern Africa from the Cape of Good Hope to the province of Natal until cultivation of the land and hunting by emigrants caused its extinction. The last known Cape lion expired in 1865. The Barbary lion, once native to all of northern Africa from Morocco to Egypt, survived into the twentieth century. The last pure member of the subspecies was shot in Morocco in 1860, although traces of the bloodlines of the Barbary are still carried by some lions in captivity. The Persian lion, which was found in Asia Minor and the Transcaucasian range, disappeared by 1930. Almost all remaining lions are now sub-Saharan African subspecies. Among the surviving African breeds are the Masai lion, which lives in central-eastern Africa. The Senegalese lion is found in western Africa. Other subspecies on the continent include the Angolan and Rhodesian lions, as well as the Transvaal lion, found in South Africa's Kruger National Park.

Despite their survival and relatively healthy numbers at this point in time, the African lions have not had an easy time of it. Like the Asiatic lions, the Africans have been the target of hunters for centuries, and have seen even their vast wilderness become tamed by an increasing human population and its need to cultivate and exploit anything in its path. Luckily for the African lion, man's increasing attention to conservation and nations' growing awareness of the value of wildlife in attracting tourists have combined to give these lions a last-minute stay of execution. Nowadays, large stretches of African wilderness are established as protected wildlife reserves or parks. Travelling in vehicles within the parks, tourists can observe lion prides going about their lives in an almost perfectly natural state.

THE LIONS OF GIR

Sadly, as we have observed, the once wide-ranging lion population has shrunk almost entirely to a few regions on a single continent, Africa. This narrowing of the lion's domain has been going on since the last century, so it is not surprising that the average person thinks of the east or central African landscape as this animal's natural homeland. But there is one remaining exception to this rule, and it is such an odd and interesting occurrence that it deserves special attention.

The Indian lion is another regional name for the Asiatic lion, or *Panthera leo persica*, the subspecies that once ranged from Greece in the west to the far eastern regions of the Indian subcontinent. This lion has played a part in the symbols and folklore of Indian culture for more than two thousand years.

The Indian lion has long been celebrated as the Lord of Beasts, and it became a symbol for human power and sovereignty. In ancient societies in India, combat with a lion was considered the ultimate test of leadership. This gradually shifted to a safer, symbolic gesture of a leader cloaking himself in or standing upon a lion skin. There were magnificent depictions of lions on the statuary at Mahabalipuram. The most important symbolic use of the lion was associated with the Emperor Asoka in Sarnath, two thousand years ago. This depiction of a lion, symbolising strength and power, eventually became the symbol for the modern Republic of India.

As India's population grew and began cultivating or settling more and more of its forest and scrublands, the Indian lion was squeezed nearly out of existence. Early in the century, the Gir Forest area in the state of Gujarat on the west coast was afflicted with a terrible famine—one so devastating that it is still mentioned in the folklore of the region. Because of the strained circumstances, the lion population began preying on the humans in the area. This prompted a massive backlash against the lions, resulting in a population of fewer than two dozen of the big cats by 1910.

Before they were completely wiped out, the Gir lions came under the protection of the Nawab of Junagadh, a local monarch who banned all lion hunting in the area. Soon, the lion population began to increase in number. By the time of Indian independence in 1947, the government had come to realise the importance and fragile nature of this last bastion of the Indian lion and the Nawab's conservation policy was upheld. Naturalists were assigned to study and take a census of the Gir's lion populace. At that time, there were more than 200 lions. Today, this number has increased to 250 lions.

The Indian government then created the Gir National Park and Lion Sanctuary, covering 540 square miles (1,404 square kilometres). The area is made up of dry scrubland with hills, rivers, and teak forest. In addition to its lion population, the Gir contains panthers, antelope, sambar, jackals, hyenas, and marsh crocodiles.

The lions of India are just slightly smaller than those of Africa, although the largest Indian lion on record was an imposing 9.6 feet (2.9 metres). The Indian lion is shaggier than its African cousin, with thicker fur on the coat and belly and a longer tail tuft. Oddly, though, the mane on the

male Indian lion is generally not as long as that of the African.

Naturalists have found no major behavioral differences between the Indian and African lions—with one important exception. The lions of Gir must share some of their territory with cattle and buffalo herdsmen. While the lions frequently attack the cattle in their midst, they have shown little aggressiveness toward humans. There are only a handful of instances of the lions coming into conflict with the local human population in the past thirty years. This is especially noteworthy considering that the park is somewhat crowded and the lions have occasionally roamed as far afield as the outskirts of nearby cities.

But this is not to say that the circumstances are ideal for the continued well-being of the Gir lions. The human population continues to encroach on the lions' territory and alter their habitat. Because the herdsmen bring their cattle through the park, their animals compete for space and food with the resident ungulate animals (largely herbivorous hoofed mammals), the lion's natural prey. Under the circumstances, the natural prey population cannot increase.

The Indian government has attempted to relieve the situation, but without much success as yet. It has erected walls around the core sanctuary to keep out grazing cattle, but this has been inef-fective. The government has attempted to relocate some of the people of the Gir, but this, too, has proven to be difficult to enforce. There have been attempts to relocate some Gir lions in other parts of India. In 1957, three of the lions were introduced into another protected area, the Chandraprabha Reserve in Uttar Pradesh. The lions did not multiply as hoped. Other lions were brought to the protected lands of the Maharajah of Varanasi, with similar results.

The most recent effort on the government's part has centred on the hills of Barda in the Porbandar region. The Indian government has set aside a 70-square-mile (182-square-kilometre) area for this potential second lion reserve. Lions had not lived in the Barda hills for more than eighty years, due to human encroachment and lack of prey animals. It will take many years before we know if the Barda will become another thriving enclave for the limited populace of Indian lions.

For now, the Gir National Park and Lion Sanctuary is the only place to see Asiatic lions in the wild, and the Indian government has begun to do more to make this unique spectacle visible to tourists and wildlife enthusiasts. The Gir Forest Department arranges weekly shows in which the lions are drawn into view with a buffalo lure. Guided Jeep safaris through the Gir are also available for observing lions. Because the lions are not afraid, or readily angered by the presence of people or vehicles, these safaris can offer very intimate views of the animals. Sometimes the lions actually approach and look over a vehicle in their midst.

As in African game reserves, the best time to observe the lions is at dawn and dusk. They are also frequently spotted following cattle being driven home, attacking any strays. The sanctuary is closed to the public from June to October. October and November are the primary mating months for the lions of Gir.

For those visitors unlucky enough not to sight a lion in the sanctuary, there is a last chance at the Junagadh Zoo at Sakar Bagh, a few miles from the centre of town. There, six Gir lions live in apparent contentment alongside tigers, leopards, and the zoo's other star attractions.

THE NATURE OF THE LION

In size, the lion is second only to the tiger among members of the cat family. The male lion's weight usually ranges from 350 to 400 pounds (157 to 180 kilogrammes), though some individuals have been as heavy as 500 pounds (225 kilo-

grammes). The female lions are 250 to 300 pounds (112.5 to 135 kilogrammes). The normal length of the male is 9 feet (2.7 metres), while the females are usually about 8 feet (2.4 metres) long.

The colouration of lions does not vary by gender. All lions are a yellowish tan colour, also described as a sandy buff. One of the advantages of this hue for the lion is that it is able to hide easily from prey among dead grasses. The lion's belly is a lighter colour, sometimes labeled as a pale cream. The lion's tail is not as heavily furred and ends in a tuft of black hair, which conceals a sharp spur that actually comprises the last few bones of the tail. The lion's ears are also covered with black hair—sometimes inadvertently exposing the beast while it is otherwise camouflaged.

The body of the lion perfectly fits the needs of a predator. Its jaws are very large and have great power. The shoulders and forelegs of the lion are another source of great strength. In fact, among cats, the lion is matched only by the tiger in the power of its limbs. The lion makes great use of the force in its legs when hunting, using blows from its paws to knock down and weaken its prey. The paws are particularly large and include long claws, used as hooks to hold victims. Because the claws retract in the paws when not in use, they maintain their sharpness. The claws are also used to aid in eating, as the lion is able to remove excessively large chunks of meat from its teeth, with the claw serving in the manner of a toothpick. The lion's tongue is also suited for helping digestion, as it is well equipped for rasping meat.

Within the lion's mouth are thirty teeth. The four largest are the razor-sharp canine teeth, with which the lion is able to grasp and kill its prey. There are also four carnassial teeth, used by the lion for cutting through tough skin and other tough parts of its food, such as tendons between muscles and bones. There are no lion teeth that are able to chew food, and so the animal must swallow its food in chunks.

Of all cats, male lions are the only ones with manes. Not all breeds of lions have the same type of mane, however. Among surviving lions of India, there are both heavy and lightly maned males, and this was also true of several of the extinct breeds of lions, such as the Barbary and Cape lions. And some of the lions of Africa, particularly those in the Serengeti, have variations in the colour and thickness of their manes. But for most males, all parts of the head, except the face, are covered with heavy, thick hair, as are the neck and the shoulders. The lion's mane is a great help during fights, because the thick hair considerably softens the blows of its foes. The male's mane is not fully grown until it reaches the age of five, though young males start to grow a little hair around their heads when they reach the age of one. The colours of the mane may vary from black to brown or yellow, with most manes having a mixture of these colours. As the lion gets older, the mane darkens.

Among the other distinguishing features of the lion are its amber eyes. They are considerably wider than the human eye, being more than 1.5 inches (37 millimetres) in diameter, compared to .9 inch (23 millimetres) of the human eye. But an even more distinctive and famous feature of the lion, and one that distinguishes it from all other species, it is loud roar. Under the right weather conditions, the lion's roar can be heard at distances of more than 5 miles (8 kilometres). To create such a sound, the lion normally needs to be standing, bending its head down slightly, and greatly expanding the chest. The roar of the lion has such power that it often stirs up great dust clouds.

Most of the roaring of the lion is done in the hour following sunset. Although roaring is such a distinctive feature, those who have spent time studying lions are still not certain of its true purpose. It could be a way of signifying control over territory. Or it could be a means of expressing contentment.

Lions make other sounds in addition to roaring. They sometimes utter low grunts as they walk along at a normal pace. They may give off a quite noticeable growl when they are angered. By contrast, a mother lion makes a soft sound when calling to her cubs.

Until recent times, it was assumed that lions did not climb trees, and it has been said that many people caught in vulnerable locations have saved themselves from lion attacks by staying in trees overnight. But further research into the subject has indeed revealed that lions do climb to very high perches in tall trees. And apparently, lions are capable of such climbing without much difficulty, because photographers who have taken pictures of lions way up in trees have noted unbent branches, indicating the ease with which the climbing occurred.

It's obvious that with the great strength of their limbs, lions are capable of springing distances both high and far. This is true even though lions are not as famous for their leaping ability as many other members of the cat family. But those who have studied lions close up have seen them jump long distances. The maximum leap of a lion has been measured at as much as 40 feet (12.1 metres). This knowledge perhaps should change the way lions are displayed in zoos and other exhibits, where they are normally kept from spectators by moats of about 30 feet (9.1 metres). It is likely that what keeps lions in those settings from jumping is their general dislike for water.

For all its majestic reputation, the lion is actually a rather lazy creature. Most of the animal's average day is spent resting.

THE LION'S WAY OF LIFE

Lions, much more so than any other members of the cat family, live sociable lives. They live in "prides", which are social structures including numerous lion members. The group can include up to thirty-five lions, but usually numbers somewhere from ten to twenty. Within this group, there are usually up to four nonpermanent males. The lionesses, who make up the bulk of the pride, along with their cubs, almost always stay in the same group for their entire lives.

Male cubs are generally expelled from the pride after three years. They either leave or are driven off by a different, usually younger, group of male lions. The cycle then repeats itself. Those driven off from a pride usually band together and roam until they reach the age of five, at which age they find a different pride, in which they are able to drive off the males and assume leadership themselves. Groups of male cats, normally numbering two to five, control the females and the territory. In the social structure of the pride, the weakest male is always thought of as higher than the strongest female.

Once they take control of a pride, the group of males works vigilantly to keep intruders, particularly other males, from disrupting the social structure. They also do not allow nonpride members to hunt in their territory. Intruders are warned to stay away from the area both by the roaring of the males and also by the liquid scent they leave on bushes. Any stranger who persists in the territory must then be ready for a violent fight. The male lions also put an end to disturbances that take place within the pride itself. The arduous nature of these tasks has resulted in the male lions only rarely

The lions in a pride can be very cooperative with one another. One example of this is the treatment of old, sick, or injured members. Healthier members often obtain food for those unable to do so.

taking part in the hunts for food, leaving most of that responsibility to the females. Studies have shown that the male lion hunts for only twelve percent of its own food; females supply it with seventy-five percent; and other predators' kills, which it simply takes, account for the remaining thirteen percent. As the percentages would indicate, male lions consume more than their fair share of kills made by females.

When the females hunt and gather food, they leave their cubs alone and abandoned in stretches that frequently last as long as forty-eight hours. Because of this, many of the cubs left behind and unprotected are often killed by hyenas, leopards, and even other lions.

Territory and Family Life

Each member of a pride does not claim its own territory, but rather all live in a single large area. A prime factor determining the size of the pride's area is the number of its members. Larger prides cover much more ground than do prides with smaller numbers. Because the range of areas inhabited by lions has become much smaller through the years, some pride territories overlap each other. This can lead to serious conflicts among the different prides, but generally the different groups are able to exist peacefully.

The degree to which food and water is plentiful determines how large an area each pride will cover. If there is abundant prey, the group usually covers an area up to 15 square miles (39 square kilometres). But if food is more difficult to obtain, the pride's territory may have to be

A lion pride often consist of two or three males and five to ten females, plus their young. Pride members generally coexist peacefully, but fights are most likely to erupt while feeding.

Two female lions are pictured in the process of bonding and grooming. Lions rub heads together to show that they mean no harm to each other. The greeting is often followed by several minutes of dedicated mutual grooming.

A resident of the Ngorongoro Crater, located within an extinct volcano, this lion lives in one of the most spectacular areas on the African continent. The crater is approximately 10 miles (16 kilometres) across and 5,000 feet (1,517 kilometres) deep.

These two females have got into a violent tussle. Fighting often occurs at mealtime, since food is divided according to the strength of each lion.

Lions do not commonly wash their own faces with their paws, the way domestic cats do. Thorough grooming by a lion is best accomplished with a social companion.

Following page:

The male members of a pride do not allow nonpride members to hunt in their territory. Intruders are warned to stay away by the roaring of the males and by a scent left on bushes.

expanded to 100 square miles (260 square kilometres). The movement of the group can also be affected by weather. During seasons of heavy rain, prey is normally scarce for the lions in the woodland areas, but much more available in the plains. This means that many of the prides have to alter their searches to cover a wider area because movements of their prey are much more erratic. During the dry season, however, pride movement is far more limited, as prey is more readily available.

The family life is generally quite a serene one, at least by the standards of the wild. There have been instances observed of lions within a pride fighting with one another, and even examples of one member of a pride killing another. However, these events are very much the exceptions, and not at all typical of lion family life. As a rule, members of the pride follow some very orderly procedures. When there is food available, lions are often able to eat peacefully without squabbling, unlike many other animals, although feeding time is the moment when fights most often occur. The reason for this is that the food is divided according to the strength of each member, with the strongest member eating the most food. The division of the meal is marked by hissing, smacking, and growling among pride members. But after eating, the lions again return to the normal tranquillity of their lives. Even members who had confrontations during the feeding will then often show affection toward one another.

Female lions produce five or six litters in a lifetime. Both the male and the female initiate mating. The female signals willingness to mate by flicking its tail and rubbing against the male. The male makes its intentions clear with a snarling grimace.

Cubs follow their mothers in quests for
food from about the age of three months.
But they do not take an active part
until they are six or seven months old.

Lions gather at a waterhole for a drink,
carefully avoiding immersing themselves
in the water, to which they have an aversion.

A pride of lionesses rests beneath a tree, saving their energy for the hunt under the cover of darkness.

Among lions, as with other species, the females are more inclined to settle down in a particular territory than the males. Female members of a lion group share a large territory rather than stake out individual domains.

Lions sleep or rest up to twenty hours a day. When they roam, they generally cover a range of about 5 miles (8 kilometres) a day. However, to procure food, they will, if need be, sometimes cover up to 15 miles (24 kilometres).

Rarely do lions gather together in the same locations of their territory, but they do know the other members of their pride, and on those occasions when they do meet, they exchange friendly greetings by rubbing cheeks, shaking heads, and grunting. The skin above the lion's eye gives off a scented secretion that pride members recognise when they rub heads with each other. The result is that all members carry a common smell by which they recognise one another.

Lions also groom each other when they meet. This is done by two lions licking the head and neck of each other. Their tongues are rough and strong and are ideally suited for cleaning and combing fur. This is needed in particular after a meal, when the lions are often covered with blood. The licking also helps remove dirt, as well as ticks and other parasites.

Most of the grooming takes place among the females and the larger cubs. The adult males do not take part in the social grooming, except on rare occasions, most likely because of the difficulty of cleaning the heavy hair of the male's mane. As for self-grooming, lions have difficulty maintaining a posture that frees paws to clean their faces. But they do keep the rest of their bodies quite clean.

Playing is another means of bonding among pride members. The male lions do not take part in much of the playing, while the females are much more frequent participants. This is another way lions are differentiated from other animals, specifically wolves and various wild dogs, whose females rarely are involved in such activities. Lionesses will playfully stalk and wrestle with other females, and they will also play considerably with cubs. This type of activity usually consists of the female poking a cub with its paw while the cub swats back, often while rolling on its back. Because they have not yet developed sufficient coordination, the youngest cubs taking part in the playing tend to do less running about and stalking, preferring just to grapple and roll about.

While most lions play in pairs, cubs also amuse themselves without companions. They often find sticks to carry and throw about, and this often leads to competitions with other cubs who try to capture the object themselves. Cubs are also known to try to play with the tufted tails of the adult males, though this frequently results in stern admonishment from their elders.

Another example of the cooperative nature of the pride is the treatment of old, sick, or injured members. Other, healthier members of the pride hunt food for those unable to do so. But when lions are old and very weak, they themselves become the prey of other carnivores, usually hyenas or wild dogs. As a result, lions in the wild do not survive to die of old age.

Lions Outside of Prides

Some males expelled from a pride do not seek to rule other prides. Instead, they continue to roam for their entire lives. They are often joined by many other younger males—who never attached themselves to prides or departed from prides at a very young age—as well as by many females, who make up about one third of the total of "nomads". Thorough research of these animals

A golden sunset on the east African plain catches this huge male lion in silhouette. Most lions are social creatures, but a percentage are unattached and nomadic.

The female lion on the rock shows little interest in the zebras and wildebeest in the background, indicating that such prey is readily available. When food becomes difficult to obtain, the territory of a lion pride expands.

in the wild has revealed that only about ten percent of these nomadic lions roam individually. The great majority of the nomads form groups, though they are much less rigid and organized than those of lion prides. Most of these groups consist of only a handful of lions. Some have as few as two members, while other groups of nomads have been documented to include as many as a dozen members, with possibly a few more.

Besides the number of members in each group, there are several other distinctions between the lions living as nomads and those living in prides. For example, there is no genetic relation between the members of a nomadic group, as there is in prides. And while many lions are part of the same pride for life, and most intruders are summarily

The colouring of lions does not vary greatly by gender. All lions are basically a yellowish tan colour, often described as a sandy buff. This colour actually serves a purpose, as it is similar in hue to dead grass and allows the lion to hide and blend in with such an environment.

The lion's diet depends on what is available in the area it inhabits. If it cannot find the prey it favors—such as zebras, antelope, and domestic livestock—it will eat whatever it can find, including fish.

The dominant male lion in a pride maintains its position for a period of about eighteen months maximum. By that time, other aspirants to the throne will have almost inevitably given him a successful challenge. The ousted lion is sometimes killed in the process.

driven off, nomadic groups are not nearly as restricted. Members arrive or depart frequently, and new associations are also formed without conflict. Many of the contacts made by nomads last just a few hours, while others endure for a few days. Nomads frequently wander in and out of several groups during a short period. There is documented evidence that some nomads make contact with a half dozen or more lions within just a couple of days. With so many different contacts, each nomad soon begins to encounter previous acquaintances, which makes it even easier to form casual groups.

One of the most likely reasons for the open nature of nomads toward each other is that most of them are not territorial. There are some nomadic groups who do defend certain land areas, but this is not the case with most of them. And because they have no particular land to defend—unlike members of a pride—they are far less hostile to intruders, and in many cases, allow strange lions to join them in social settings and even to partake of meals.

Apparently, lions who are not territorial are much more tolerant of other lions, and studies in the wild have shown that though it may take some persistence, a nomad may well be accepted almost peacefully by other unattached lions and allowed to become a member of the casually formed and allied group.

This female lion is on the hunt. As lionesses hunt and gather food, they leave their cubs alone for periods as long as forty-eight hours. Because of this, many cubs left behind and unprotected are killed by hyenas, leopards, and even other lions.

Most lions live within a very structured social unit. An intruder into the family unit is often violently challenged. The fights that erupt sometimes prove fatal for the nonpride lion.

Lions often groom each other—a particularly practical habit after a meal, when the animals are often covered with blood. Mutual licking also helps remove dirt, as well as ticks and other parasites.

Because of the lack of good cover in scrub areas, the lion often has trouble catching its prey in daytime or on a night with a full moon. Prey can often detect the lion's presence from hundreds of yards away, enabling it to escape.

REPRODUCTION

Lions tend to breed throughout the year, though there are some patterns that have been observed. In the wilds of the Serengeti, as well as in South Africa's Kruger National Park, most breeding takes place from March to June. In western Africa, as well as India, the lions tend to breed from October to December. If the female does not become pregnant during these periods, another breeding cycle usually occurs within three months. During the times of mating, males and females are together constantly. The lionesses are in heat from four to eight days. Lions have been known to mate forty times a day, although even higher numbers have been counted. In a German zoo, two paired lions mated more than three hundred times in a week-long period. The actual mating itself only lasts about six seconds, which often concludes with the male lightly biting the female's neck, to which the female usually responds with a swing of her paw and a low growl.

The Role of Genetics

All the female members of a pride are closely related to each other, since all new members are the daughters, granddaughters, aunts, or nieces of the lionesses they replace. This means that all the offspring of the pride are also closely related, and so the male members who are driven out of a pride and take over another group are

Cubs stay dependent on their mothers for some time—often more than two years. When their mothers next mate, however, the cubs must fend for themselves. Lions reach their full size and strength by the age of five or six.

A male and female lion are shown in the act of mating. Because the lioness may mate with more than one male, it is biologically possible that members of the same litter may have different fathers.

also usually full brothers from the same litter. Because the female lion may mate with more than one male, it is biologically possible that members of the same litter have different fathers. There is also a chance that the partnered males of a pride may not have the same mother, although, almost always coming from the same pride, they are related, even if distantly. In sum, the males who are companions in controlling a pride may be full brothers or they may only be distant cousins, while all the females are usually closely related. However, the females are not related to the males, and this allows for a greater genetic mixture.

The manner in which males take over a pride through superior strength is one of the ways lions are able to improve the breed with each passing generation. The superior genes of the conquering males, which make them capable of taking over the pride, are bred into their offspring, as are the superior hunting skills of the prospering lionesses. The stability required by the females to rear their cubs successfully is also evident genetically and bred into subsequent generations. By the process of natural selection, the superior genes of the able male and female become more common with each passing generation, gradually decreasing the less productive parts within the genetic mixture of the species. Through this process, lions are able to continually produce high-quality replicas of themselves.

Though it may appear otherwise, this female lion is actually getting in the mood for mating. Growling, pawing, and biting are typical elements in a lion's mating dance.

In some areas, such as Ngorongoro Crater in Tanzania, lion prides are harmed by inbreeding. This occurs because a locale like the crater—difficult to reach from areas beyond—decreases the number of outsiders coming into a pride's gene pool.

Following page:

It is generally believed that lion cubs are blind at birth and that their eyes do not open for two to three weeks. But cubs have been observed opening their eyes even earlier.

Lions tend to breed throughout the year, though patterns do occur from pride to pride and place to place. In the national parks Serengeti and Kruger, for instance, most breeding takes place in the months of March to June.

A pair of lions engages in the mating ritual, complete with elements of violence. The manner in which male lions take over a pride through superior strength is one way that lions may improve the breed with each successive generation.

Actual mating between male and female lions lasts about six seconds. The encounter often concludes with the male lightly biting the female's neck.

Are lionesses good or bad mothers? The only conclusive answer, really, is a little of both. On some occasions, they defend their cubs to the death. At other times, lionesses neglect their young—possibly to the extent that they die.

Giving Birth

The gestation period for the female is between 105 and 115 days. When ready to give birth, the female seeks a site that provides protection from such factors as cold, excessive sunlight, wind, and moisture. In the dry season, most lionesses give birth near rivers or reeds. In the rainy season, the pregnant lioness seeks higher ground amid rocks or suitable spots in hills. Not only must the spot secured provide protection from nature and access to water, but it must also camouflage cubs from enemies. There may be occasions when the mother moves the location, and when it does so, it moves the cubs one at a time, carrying them in the mouth.

Most lionesses have litters of two to four, although in captivity some have had as many as nine. In the wild, it is unlikely that more than four cubs could survive: Since the mother has only four nipples, more than four cubs could not obtain sufficient nutrition. If more than four cubs were born in the wild, the stronger ones would soon outdistance the weaker siblings.

Seen here, a female lion and cubs feed on a hartebeest kill. Younger members of a lion pride drive the prey into a kind of ambush, while the lionesses make the kill.

The period when
a lion cub begins
teething can be
very dangerous.
The appearance
of permanent teeth
brings with it a
great deal of pain,
leaving the cubs
subject to infections
and fevers.

At birth, each cub is about 1 foot (30.5 centimeters) long and weighs about 1 pound (.45 kilogram). When they are born, lion cubs are already covered with fur and have some gray spots of varying shapes. They are also born with a wide, untufted tail. It is generally believed that lion cubs are blind at birth, and their eyes do not open for two to three weeks, though there have been examples spotted of eyes opening earlier. There is no evidence, though, that the cub's eyesight functions until three to four weeks after birth. Their milk teeth first appear about three weeks after birth, and they are able to start eating meat about one week later.

All the female members of a pride are closely related to each other, since all new members are the daughters, granddaughters, aunts, or nieces of the lionesses they replace.

Raising Cubs

After giving birth, a mother lion stays away from the other members of the pride for about six weeks before rejoining the group, with cubs in tow. When the cubs are old enough to move about on their own, several mothers often form a group. The responsibility of caring for the cubs is then shared by all the mothers. The cubs in this group do not just nurse on their own mother, but on anyone who is available. And the mothers protect all of the cubs as if they were their own. It is also not unusual for a female without cubs but with the pride also to shield and care for the cubs.

At birth, cubs are about 1 foot (30.5 centimetres) long and weigh in the area of 1 pound (.45 kilogramme). When they are born, the cubs are already covered with fur and have grey spots of varying shapes.

The male lions in the pride also tolerate the cubs—even when the youngsters play with their food and even try to take food out of the adults' mouths. At most, the males show their disapproval to the young ones with a hissing sound.

Cubs begin to follow their mothers in quests for food at about the age of three months. But they do not take part actively until after they are weaned from the mothers, usually in their sixth or seventh months. Before that, their role in the hunting forays is more one of watching and stumbling along. A most dangerous time for the maturing lions occurs in the period between their ninth and twelfth months, when their permanent teeth first appear,

Lion cubs spend a lot of their time at play, grappling with and swatting one another. Their pawing and wrestling resembles the play of domestic kittens.

A mother lion is not entirely selfless.
When food is scarce, the lioness will take
care of its own needs before those of the cubs.

Although they have demonstrated a capacity for producing larger litters in captivity, a lioness seldom has more than four cubs at a time, for very practical reasons. Since the mother has only four nipples, more than four cubs could not obtain sufficient nutrition.

Though several lion cubs may die in a litter, the number that survives is sufficient to maintain a typical group's continued existence. Cubs born to nomadic lionesses have a harder time surviving.

In the wild, most female lions have
litters of from two to four cubs.
In captivity, this number has increased
considerably, with some lionesses
having as many as nine in a single litter.

On a family outing, lionesses and their cubs
gather at a waterhole. A lioness stays away from
other members of the pride for around six weeks
after giving birth. It then rejoins the group.

When cubs are old enough to move about
on their own, several mother lionesses may
form a group. The responsibility for caring
for the cubs is then shared by all the mothers.

When a female lion gives birth, it generally keeps the
litter in a hiding place away from the rest of the pride.

Playing is an important social activity among lions. Adult males do not often take part in this, but lionesses and cubs play frequently. The animals stalk and chase each other, especially in the hours of dawn and dusk.

bringing with them a great deal of pain. The cubs in this period are subject to infections and fevers, as well as a dangerous level of restlessness. For these reasons, there is a high mortality rate during this period.

Most of the lions who survive the dangers and rigours of their first year continue to hunt with their mothers for quite some time, often more than two years. Mothers leave their offspring to fend for themselves when they next mate. Lionesses do not have another litter until their previous cubs are at least one and a half to two years old. They do not have offspring with them of varying ages, so the more mature cubs who have left their mothers tend to band together for awhile, until they reach their own sexual maturity, usually at age four. At that age, the males start to establish their own territories. The lion finally reaches its full size at age four.

At the Masai Mara Game Reserve in Kenya, this cub rests away from the midday sun. The cub's mother is visible in the background, resting but ready to defend its young in a moment if there is trouble.

Following page:

When they leave their mothers, lion cubs tend to band together, at least until they reach their sexual maturity. This occurs at around the age of four.

There is a very high rate of mortality for lion cubs born in the wild. In some studies, as many as sixty percent of the cubs died before reaching maturity.

A pair of Kenyan lion cubs is pictured at play. While most cubs play in pairs, the young ones also amuse themselves without companions.

Most of the lion cubs who survive the dangers and rigors of their first year in the wild continue to hunt with their mothers for some time, often for more than two years.

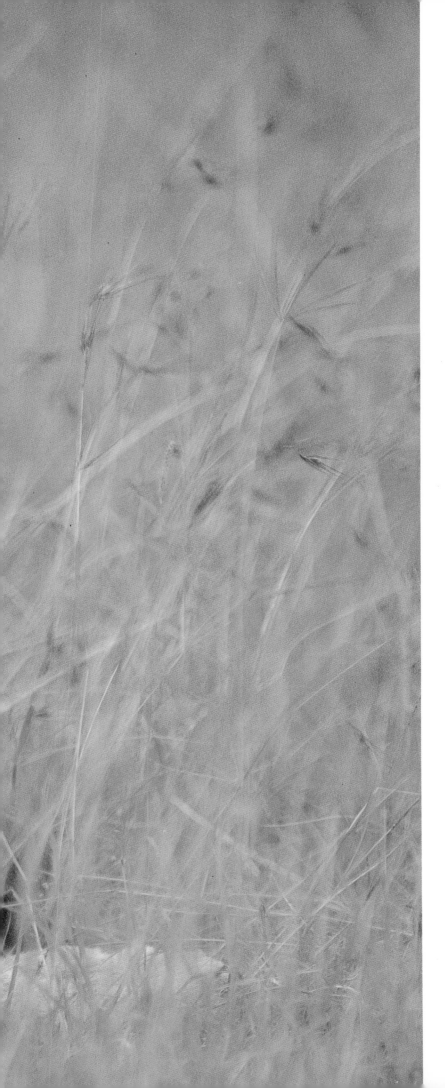

HUNTING

The choice of animals that the lion hunts for food is dependent on what is available in their areas of habitation. Generally, the scrub areas in which the lions live provide many animals who live off the vegetation of the region. These herbivorous animals—wildebeest, zebras, antelope, gazelles, and waterbuck—are the lion's primary sources of prey. They also have a fondness for warthogs, and have been known to wait many hours for them to emerge from holes in the ground. If a lion is hungry enough and otherwise not able to find food, it will also eat whatever it can find, including fish. Other larger animals are also hunted by lions, including buffalo and giraffes, though it is much more difficult for the lions to succeed in their attacks against these stronger creatures. Many lions have been injured trying to control the bigger animals. It's common after such an encounter for an injured lion to be unable to take part in any future hunts.

Most hunting done by lions is under a cover of darkness, when there is much less chance for them to be detected. It is common for the lions to observe their prey during daylight hours, usually soon before sunset. But they then wait until dark before attacking. Similarly, if there is bright moonlight, lions wait until it is obscured before they commence their hunts. Much of the reason for this is the lack of cover they have in their scrub areas of habitation. Often in the daytime, a lion will start to close in on a potential victim, but will be detected by its prey, who is then able to escape. Those lions who live in areas with more dense vegetation, however, are able to do more hunting in the daytime. Other hunting that occurs

A female lion guards its wildebeest kill. The lion's prey can depend on a number of natural factors. In some lion reserves, the wildebeest, for example, is not available during the dry season, when it migrates to the north.

This female has made its kill. In the Ngorongoro Crater, where this photograph was taken, geographical boundaries contain the wildlife, making prey plentiful and easy to catch.

The scrub areas in which most lions live provide prey in the form of herbivorous animals—wildebeest, zebras, antelope, gazelles, and waterbuck, among them.

Lions often make hunting for food a cooperative effort. In an attack, several lions encircle a herd, driving the victims into other lions, which await in the tall grass.

in sunlight is in relation to the activity of the lion's prey. When zebras or gazelles drink from lakes or rivers during the day, their presence often produces a flurry of hunting. But generally, most stalking by lions is done just after sunset, or, more commonly, in the middle of the night, several hours before dawn.

More than any of their other senses, lions use their sight to help them hunt. Lions observed under vegetative cover waiting to pounce give clear indications that their main way of following their prey is through vision. The best indication of this is when lions stick their heads up high out of their cover in order to follow the animal they are stalking. In the process they sometimes give themselves away. Final pursuit of a victim is also done strictly by sight.

Lions sometimes detect prey using their hearing. They frequently react to the sounds of animals walking or moving through water and set out to investigate. There have also been some examples of lions utilising their sense of smell to aid in hunting. But generally, lions only hunt what they see, and they are not considered particularly adept at detecting prey. It is quite normal for a large group of potential victims to pass by during the day and not be noticed by sleeping lions.

In addition to the fact that their senses are not especially sharp, there are several other reasons that lions are not as proficient at hunting as other predators. Not only do they occasionally give away their cover, but they also pay little attention to the wind's direction, which frequently allows

A charging lion can reach speeds of close to 40 miles (64 kilometres) per hour. When a group of lions hunts together, its tactics are scientific and ruthless. The group encircles the prey, knocks it down, and then grabs and suffocates it.

At one time, the Indian lion could be found in a wide area across the northern part of the sub-continent. Today the 116 square miles (302 square kilometres) of Gir National Park and Lion Sanctuary is the only remaining home for the Asiatic animal.

It is lions versus warthog in this scene from the plains of Kenya. Most of a lion's prey can outrun it, so the big cat must stalk to within 100 feet (30.3 metres) before charging.

The bloody muzzle of this lioness indicates it recently made a kill. Greatly outnumbered by the animals upon which they prey—particularly herbivores—lions tend to actively hunt only one out of every fifteen types of species in their habitat.

their scent to be carried ahead, alerting potential prey to danger. However, despite some of the inefficiencies, prey is so plentiful in most of their current areas of existence that they are able to overcome these shortcomings. In their domains of eastern and central Africa, the lions are greatly outnumbered by the herbivores they hunt. Generally, they kill off about one out of fifteen of the zebras, gazelles, and other animals of the area. So the lions not only do not have much effect on the populations of their prey, but they also don't even help to control their numbers. The herbivores taken by lions through much of Africa only represent the amount that would be lost in the region's next drought.

In addition to the plentiful supply of quarry, other factors also help to make up for some of the lion's hunting deficiencies. Its inattentiveness to the wind often does not discourage

The lion is the largest of the African carnivores. While most of its prey is of medium size, it hunts and attacks anything from the tiny rodent to the enormous buffalo.

Lions descend on a buffalo kill, while other members of the buffalo herd look on helplessly. Though the lion triumphed in this confrontation, the buffalo, especially when wounded, is a fierce fighter. Indeed, many lions have been killed in battle with these sturdy animals.

This animal is stalking its dinner. Those lions who live in areas with more dense vegetation than the usual scrub are able to do more of their hunting in the daytime because they are more easily camouflaged.

While it is often written that male lions leave the primary hunting to the females out of arrogance or laziness, the male's heavy mane may have something to do with it as well. The mane makes stalking prey more difficult because it can be so easily spotted.

More than any of their other senses, lions use sight to help them hunt. Lions observed under cover waiting to pounce give clear indications that their principal way of following their prey is through vision.

Pictured in midhunt, a Kenyan lion closes in on its wildebeest prey.

Following page:

The average prey of a lion weighs about 250 pounds (112.5 kilogrammes). From this carcass, the lion obtains a meal of about 40 pounds (18 kilogrammes). Lions do not eat daily, although they have been known to hunt on days when they do not eat.

Lions often hunt alone, but also work cooperatively with several pride members to take on larger and stronger prey. During the attack, one lion suffocates the prey while the others move in to tear it open.

A lioness feeds on a buffalo kill. When females bring back food for the pride, the male lions take more than their fair share. About seventy-five percent of male lions' food comes from prey obtained by females.

An adult male drags a killed wildebeest across the dry grassland in the Masai Mara Game Reserve in Kenya. Every summer, millions of wildebeest migrate there from the drier regions of the south, keeping the lion population well fed.

One of the rare Asiatic lions of Gir National Park and Lion Sanctuary in India displays a bloody muzzle. The Asiatic lion is slightly smaller than the African type and has demonstrated a greater ability to coexist with humans.

potential prey from coming into sight, because during certain months of the year, the scent of lions is detectable by other wildlife throughout much of the region, especially by rivers or streams. So it would be impractical for gazelles or other herbivores to avoid water because they've picked up a lion scent.

Another, even more important reason that lions are able to find enough food is that they usually do their hunting in cooperation. They will stalk their victims for fifteen minutes up to an hour before pouncing. Normally, several lions circle around a herd they are attacking, driving their victims toward other lions hiding in tall grasses. These lions then attack their prey from the sides or from behind. This type of cooperative hunting also makes up for another notable problem that lions have, at least compared to many other predators: their lack of speed. Although lions are not slow,

Most hunting by lions is done under cover of darkness, when there is much less chance of their being detected. The lion pictured is stalking prey.

their maximum speed is about 30 miles (48 kilometres) per hour.

In addition, stamina is another problem for lions. They rarely run after another animal for more than 100 yards (91 metres). But by working in groups, they are able to capture prey that would otherwise be too fast or too elusive for them to catch.

Another advantage lions gain through group hunting is that when they have killed an animal too large for one to eat alone, several can take part in the eating. This not only gives food to more lions at one time, but also lets them avoid the problem of storing or guarding their food. Other members of the cat family, such as leopards or tigers, either hide their victims in trees or remain in the vicinity until they finish eating the carcass. Unlike the inhabitants of the jungles and forests, the lions in their scrublands would not be able to hide their food or shelter it.

Lions do not eat every day, although they have been known to hunt on days they don't eat. When a lion starts to eat, it usually begins with its victim's intestines, which is the most nutritious part of the meal. After that, the lion consumes the meat of the carcass, usually working forward from the hindquarters. The average prey of a lion weighs about 250 pounds (112.5 kilogrammes), from which each lion obtains a meal of about 40 pounds (18 kilogrammes).

If lions have had a really big meal, they usually rest for at least twenty-four hours. This is fairly common, because lions tend to consume whatever food they have, eating as much as 75 pounds (34 kilogrammes) of meat at one time. Prides have been observed gorging themselves for several hours and then moving very little for as many as four days. By the fifth day, they begin to walk around; by the sixth day, they are again ready to look for food.

The Masai Mara Game Reserve, established in 1961, is one of the best locations in the world for viewing big game in the wild. Among other facilities, the reserve offers visitors the chance to observe animals from hot-air balloons.

A male African lion transports an unusual prey—a crocodile. Crocodiles inhabit the pools in many game reserves, such as Nairobi National Park. The largest of the Nile crocodiles, growing to 16 feet (4.8 meters) in length, would not be easily vanquished by a lion.

This female lion, pictured with zebra prey, seems to be wondering if the photographer has designs on its dinner.

During a year's time, the hunting lion may kill about twenty animals. After the animal kills its prey, it is likely to begin eating the intestines, the most nutritious part of the menu.

THE LION AND MAN

The relationship between man and lion has been a significant one almost since the beginning of recorded history. Poets and artists, as well as royalty, rulers, and religious leaders, have long recognized the symbolic power of the King of Beasts.

Egyptian pharaohs and Assyrian kings kept lions as companions. Legend has it that these lions were trained to hunt and rode into battle with their royal masters. Ramses II, it has been written, went into combat with his prized great cat sharing his chariot.

Other rulers had crueller uses for their captive lions. In ancient Rome, lions were the wild beasts of choice for various horrible blood sports. In the great coliseums of Rome and elsewhere in the Empire, starved, maddened lions were pitted against each other or against equally desperate tigers and fought to the death for the amusement of spectators.

Still more bloody entertainment was provided by pitting lions against humans—either defenseless condemned prisoners (the early Christian martyrs among them), who were literally fed to the starving cats, or armed slaves and gladiators, who fought for freedom or riches. This latter spectacle has been immortalised in numerous histories, novels, and motion pictures. Such events would draw huge crowds of thirty thousand or more. The animals were kept in stone and

The lion's mane takes five years to fully develop. Young male lions begin to grow the mane at the age of one year, with a small crop of hair showing around the head at that time.

A lion track imprinted in the sands of the Kalahari Desert illustrates the impressive size of this animal's feet. The lion's huge front paws enable it to slap down prey with a brutal force.

As the spread of human populations overwhelmed them, lions were systematically eliminated from various parts of the world. Included in this group is the Barbary lion, which once roamed from Morocco to Egypt.

For nearly a century, Kenya allowed the nearly unrestricted hunting of lions for profit or sport. But by the 1970s, the country no longer tolerated poachers and trophy hunters. In 1977, Kenya made all lion hunting illegal.

steel cages, their fury rising as raw meat was dangled before them, always out of reach, and clubs descended on their heads.

The lion's designation as the King of Beasts can be traced back to writings from the first century. Lions were frequently part of royal family crests and coats-of-arms for the kingdoms of England, Scotland, Norway, Denmark, Wales, and Luxembourg. Richard I, the twelfth-century English king and veteran of the Crusades to the Holy Land, was dubbed Richard Coeur de Lion, or Richard the Lion Hearted, for his bravery in battle. The lion was frequently depicted as a symbol of power and strength in various parts of Asia—even in China, to which it is not indigenous.

The Lion on Display

In 1720, an African lion was the first foreign wild animal to be put on exhibit in North America. The exhibit caused a sizable commotion wherever it went. The owners used their lion exhibit to sell buttons and patent medicines. Following in the ancient tradition of rulers keeping lions at their side, American President Andrew Jackson accepted one of the big cats as a present from the Emperor of Morocco in 1830.

It was in the early nineteenth century that the first large-scale travelling circuses began to thrive in Europe and the United States. As in Ancient Rome, lions—typically billed as "Snarling Man-Eaters from Darkest Africa!"—were the highlighted stars of these spectacles, but unlike the Roman circus lions, these were not expected to maim and devour human beings at every performance. The key to a circus lion act was to make it seem as dangerous and exciting as possible without anyone actually being hurt. Skilled lion trainers, or "tamers", became international celebrities. The most notable of these early lion trainer stars was Isaac Van Amburgh, whose famous show was called the Grand Spectacle of Charlemagne. To the children and adults of several continents, he was known as the Greatest Lion Tamer in the World. Van Amburgh put on his lion act in legitimate theatres, as well as circus bigtops, and in 1839 he and Charlemagne, his lion, performed for England's Queen Victoria.

As the size and popularity of circuses grew, so too did their lion populations. The traveling show of P.T. Barnum in the 1850s—called Barnum's Great Asiatic Carnival, Museum and Menagerie—included up to ten lions in its featured act. Although tigers were an equally tempting attraction for most circus-goers, the Indian cats were much scarcer, being more expensive to import and more difficult to breed in captivity.

With no scientific manual for the training of wild animals, the early lion tamers learned their trade through a dangerous process of trial and error. In the first epoch of circus lion acts, the ideal was to present the animals in highly disciplined and formal tableaux, awing the audience with the sight of a human taming ferocious, man-eating beasts. But by the early twentieth century, American lion trainers were pioneering a new, more dangerous, and decidedly more exciting type of act. These trainers brought a glimpse of the violence of the African wilds, and a bit of the blood lust of the old Roman arenas, into the bigtop tents. The lion act became a frenzied drama, with groups of big cats wrathfully pacing the ringed enclosure, their trainer weaving among them with whip and upturned chair.

An African male lion engages in its most legendary characteristic behaviour, a full-blooded roar. No one who hears that ground-quaking noise in person is ever likely to forget it.

A large African male lion is pictured resting. The lion's colouring allows it to blend in with the sandy-coloured plain. The animal's belly is lighter than its top, which is a pale cream colour.

The lion's mane is a great help during fights, because the thick growth of hair softens the blows of its foes.

A young adult female is pictured stretching. Although lions generally cover a range of about 5 miles (8 kilometres) in a day, they may cover three or four times that ground, if necessary, to obtain food.

Hearing the lions's roar on a recording does not prepare one for the vibrating force and power of a live encounter with this mighty sound.

Circuses reached their peak of popularity in the early twentieth century, with hundreds of different units, large and small, crisscrossing North America and Europe: the Cole Bros., Kelly-Miller, Sells-Floto, Al G. Barnes, Howe's Great London, Clyde Beatty, and, of course, Ringling Bros. and Barnum & Bailey, to name a few. Lion acts remained the leading attraction for most of these circuses, featuring as many as forty big cats in the ring at one time.

With so much competition, animal trainers were continually trying to increase the spectacle and danger in their acts. In the late 1890s, the European trainer Herman Weedon was the first to combine in one cage those traditional enemies, the lion and tiger. Other trainers followed his lead, intensifying their acts with hate-filled, danger-laden combinations from Africa and India.

While most trainers believed they were actually safer in a cage with a mixed-cat group (because the lions and tigers would be too preoccupied with each other to turn on the trainer), events inside the ring always had the potential to go completely out of control.

It is common practice for a lion to observe its prey during daylight hours, usually just before sunset. But the actual stalking and kill does not occur until darkness has fallen.

Lions reach maturity when they are between three and four years old. In the wild, the average life expectancy is about a decade. Pictured is a veteran lion on the Kenyan plain.

Previous page:

Even in the so-called wild, it is difficult for animals to escape signs of human encroachment. These lions are seen crossing the well-established tracks of an automobile path.

The Safari Years

While lions in captivity suffered confinement and humiliation and occasional abuse, many of the cats in the wild did not fare any better. The lion populations in Europe, Asia, and North Africa, as noted earlier, were almost entirely wiped out by hunting and human encroachment of their habitat. For all the symbolic value placed on the lion in the abstract, lions in the wild were effectively demonised as bloodthirsty man-eaters. Of course, in many of these cases it was only to be expected that the King of Beasts would put up a fierce fight when confronted with rifle-bearing intruders.

In the late nineteenth century, the time of the great African explorers, there were few who did not recount hair-raising encounters with a lion or two. Dr. David Livingstone had a near-fatal run-in while trying to help a group of Tswana tribesmen dispose of one rogue lion in the northern Transvaal. The traditional tribal method for trapping the animal involved spears and long fans made of bright ostrich feathers. As the hunters encircled and closed in on the lion, they would use the fans like matadors' capes, distracting and disorientating their quarry. On this occasion, the lion charged through the circle and hid in the nearby grass. As the group fanned out to search for the lion, Dr. Livingstone unfortunately stumbled upon its hiding place. Livingstone fired as the cat charged. The lion knocked the doctor flat on the ground, then climbed over him, took an arm in its mouth, and broke it. Livingstone was shaken so violently that he passed out. The lion was in the process of

These lions are about to make dinner out of an unlucky warthog. African lions were once routinely hunted and killed by tourists on safari. These days, the tourist is much more likely to watch the lion kill its prey.

dragging the doctor away when the tribesmen caught up and managed to kill it. The injury to Dr. Livingstone's arm plagued him for the rest of his life.

As the late nineteenth century in Africa was the era of exploration, the early twentieth century years were the time of the great hunting safaris (*safari* being a Swahili word for "voyage"). The change reflected the impact of colonialism. In less than twenty years, European claims on Africa went from ten percent of the total land mass to ninety percent. This brought tens of thousands of new settlers to the east African territories, and many of them were sportsmen and hunters, or at any rate eager to take a crack at the lion. The invention of inexpensive hunting rifles at the time made big-game hunting affordable for almost every European resident or visitor.

The growing number of newcomers and inexperienced hunters wishing to go into the wilderness

Once native to massive regions of Africa and the Middle East, lions were hunted down as human populations spread into their areas of existence. As a result, several subspecies of lions are now extinct.

Young male lions leave the pride within four to six months after reaching three years of age. They are then replaced by other males.

produced a need for professional hunters for hire. The safaris themselves grew to absurdly elaborate proportions, involving scores of bearers and supplies that ranged from portable bathtubs to pianos. The first-class African safari became de rigueur for the rich and powerful. Among those notables who went on lengthy lion-hunting safaris were the Prince of Wales, Lord Randolph Churchill, and U.S. President Theodore Roosevelt. Roosevelt's 1908 safari, recounted in his subsequent book, *African Game Trails*, did the most to popularise the large-scale African hunting expedition. The safari cost a staggering amount of money and involved a caravan of wagons, animals, and bearers stretched out for over 1 mile (1.6 kilometres) whilst on the move.

Roosevelt hunted the lion after the style of his adviser, Sir Alfred Pease, chasing the big cat down on horseback and then confronting it on foot for the kill. Roosevelt shot seventeen lions on this first safari—along with nearly five hundred other animals.

Some years later, writer Ernest Hemingway contributed to the romantic image of the big-game safari in such works as *The Snows of Kilimanjaro* and *The Green Hills of Africa*, based on his own experiences and observations in Africa. The lion hunt, in Hemingway's fictitious world, was a symbolic rite, the ultimate test of masculine courage.

On a less metaphoric—and less authoritative—level, Hollywood romanticised the safari as equal parts adventure and adultery. Lions were routinely, if excitingly, dispatched in these films, always

A beautiful female lion wades through a marsh in search of food. Lions enter water when necessary, but they do not particularly like it.

A lion may sometimes rest or sleep for an entire day after having a very big meal. This is understandable when one considers that a lion can gorge itself on as much as 75 pounds (34 kilogrammes) of meat at one time.

The body of the lion perfectly fits the needs of a predatory animal. Its jaws are very large and powerful. Among cats, only the tiger has a more powerful bite.

while furiously charging the hunters. Tarzan, Edgar Rice Burroughs' fictitious hero raised by African apes, was shown on screen in hand-to-hand combat with the lion. Tarzan was always the somewhat unlikely victor in these contests. The tamed, captive lions used in these movies were usually toothless senior citizens, and probably still capable of killing a stunt man with one blow of the paw if they weren't being such good sports about the absurd proceedings.

While writers and moviemakers glamourised the ritualised stalking and shooting of the lions, the reality was something else again. On actual safaris, the amateur lion hunters would frequently not make clean kills, wounding the cats and leaving them to the mercy of scavengers. Some hunters went after lions with packs of killer dogs. Although the east African authorities were strict about issuing limited-kill licences for hunting elephants and other big game, lion hunting required no licensing at all: The King of Beasts ranked as vermin, to be killed at will without any need for authorisation or limitations.

There is no way of calculating how many lions were killed in the fifty- or sixty-year "golden age" of the African safari, but it undoubtedly played an enormous part in the depletion of the overall lion population.

The Story of Elsa

The legendary Elsa of *Born Free* fame showed once and for all that lions are in fact adaptable and capable of crossing the boundaries between civilisation and wilderness without dire consequences. It is a story worth recounting, as it did much to disprove negative perceptions of the lion.

The story begins with George Adamson, who became a game warden in Kenya in 1938. As the administrator of an expansive area of over 100,000 square miles (260,000 square kilometres), which extended from Mount Kenya to the Abyssinian border, Adamson had the primary responsibilities of preventing poaching and taking care of animals in the area who posed threats to the people. In 1956, while seeking out a man-eating lion residing amid some hills in the region, Adamson was forced to kill a lion that attacked his group. It was only after the lion's death that Adamson sadly realized it was a nursing mother, and eventually he found its three lion cubs, which were hidden in a rock opening. He returned them to his camp, where he and his wife, Joy, began to raise them.

One of the lion's titles, King of the Jungle, is a misnomer. Most lions, such as this Kenyan male, live in grassy plains areas. They can exist both in colder areas and very hot regions.

Of the lion's thirty teeth, four canines are used for grasping and killing its prey. Four cheek teeth are used for cutting through tough skin and other tough parts of its food, such as tendons between muscles and bones.

Lions are not as proficient at hunting as many other predators. They reveal their cover at times, giving their prey time to escape, and pay little heed to the wind, allowing their scent to be carried ahead.

All three of the cubs were female, and, since they were only a few days old when they were retrieved, they had not yet opened their eyes. After a couple of days, Joy Adamson was able to get them to accept the unsweetened milk she offered them through a rubber tube. Soon, supplies arrived at the Adamson camp from the nearest African market, with more milk for the cubs, along with cod liver oil, glucose, and baby bottles. The cubs grew and soon began to partake of the normal lion recreations. They would stalk each other in the playful manner of lions living in prides in the wild, but with no adult lions around, they incorporated the humans at the camp into their activities, jumping on their backs as if hunting in the wild. The cubs would also climb trees, though often with such voraciousness that they ended up on too high a perch and needed to be rescued.

Their human handlers soon found out that the three female cubs all had distinctly recognisable personalities. Joy Adamson named one of them The Big One, another The Jolly One, and the third Elsa, after a friend of hers with a lively personality. If the three cubs had been raised in the wild, Elsa, being the smallest and weakest of the group, probably would not have been able to survive. But with the help of the Adamsons and the others in the camp, the cub not only survived but eventually prospered. The two stronger cubs were less reliant on handlers than was Elsa, and so they were sent to a zoo in Rotterdam, where they lived happily and luxuriously.

Elsa began to accompany the Adamsons on safaris in the wild. They travelled to many different areas of the continent. When Elsa was about two years old, the Adamsons allowed her to go off repeatedly on her own. Elsa did make other lion acquaintances. A half year later, the Adamsons decided to release Elsa back into the wild—an experiment that had never been attempted before with a lion raised by humans.

It was not easy, however, to wean Elsa from her human handlers. They attempted to show her how to hunt and kill, yet Elsa seemed reluctant to leave the couple to live entirely in the wild. She even became quite ill at one point. Eventually, the Adamsons found a different location for Elsa to live in—with a better climate, more accessible supplies of water, and no danger of hunters. In her new surroundings, the lion developed some hunting skills.

Finally, Elsa was able to be left on her own for a week. When the Adamsons returned to check on her, they found that her stomach was full, meaning she had eaten recently. Soon she took on a male lion partner. Eventually, as Elsa became more a part of nature with each day, she seemed all but ready to forgo all her great human friends in favor of her new, "natural" way of life.

As time went by, the Adamsons would still visit Elsa's area about every three weeks, firing off a shot to let her know they had arrived. Elsa would normally come into camp within a few hours and stay with the Adamsons for a few days. Amazingly, she was able to continue living in the wild whilst maintaining a relationship with the couple. They would always give her some meat on her arrival. When the Adamsons would be ready to leave, Elsa after showing much affection, would follow a routine of aloofness to lessen the pain of separation. The lion finally was able to lead an independent life.

The incredible experiment was a complete success. And it was made even more so when, late in 1959, Elsa gave birth to a litter of cubs. *Born Free*, written by Joy Adamson and published in 1960, chronicled the entire story. It startled the scientific community to the same extent that it entertained millions of readers.

The lion's differently shaped teeth are variously equipped for holding, killing, and cutting. As the lion has no teeth with which to chew, it must swallow food in large chunks.

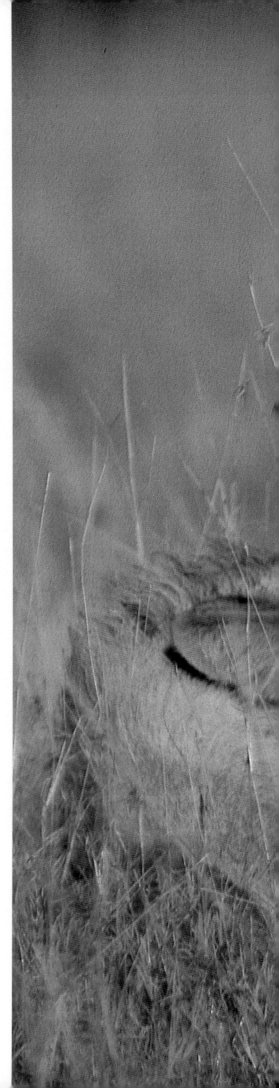

This fellow, a resident of the Amboseli National Park in Kenya, is showing why it is not a good idea to get within biting range of a wild lion: It is equipped with thirty teeth, some as sharp as razors.

Young male lions leave the pride within four to six months after reaching three years of age. They are then replaced by other males.

A TOUR OF LION COUNTRY

Progress and human overpopulation in this century have not mixed well with nature or wildlife. The roll call of vanished wilderness and extinct or endangered animals is a long one and still growing. The continent of Africa has faced this problem as much as any other. The usual elements—human encroachment, alteration or destruction of habitat, famine, excessive hunting, and poaching—have wiped once thriving species off the map in numerous regions of Africa.

At one time not many years ago, the world faced a future where such magnificent creatures as the elephant and the lion would no longer exist in the wild. Luckily, this situation was halted if not entirely reversed, by a combination of factors, from the growing strength of the conservation and ecology movement to African nations' awareness of the value of wildlife as a tourist attraction. In the past thirty years, the countries of Africa have gone to great efforts to reserve and protect their wildlife populations.

Now there are dozens of nationally sponsored game parks and reserves where the animal life thrives almost as it did before the arrival of civilisation. In Kenya alone there are more than forty such areas. In most of these, there are facilities and accommodations for visitors on photographic "safaris" (the days of the huge hunting expeditions by tourists are now almost entirely illegal in the big-game regions of Africa).

Still, it is worth noting that no matter how large some of these animal reserves may appear to be, they are only a fraction of the land these animals once roamed freely. Kenya's vast system of national parks adds up to just over seven percent of the nation's total land area.

Because lions cannot adequately chew food, chunks sometimes remain their teeth. The claws are then used in the manner of a toothpick to loosen these pieces.

Each part of the lion's body aids its ability as a carnivorous hunter. Its jaws, teeth, shoulders, and legs are all sources of great strength. The paws are particularly large and are used to subdue prey.

Shimba Hills National Park is one of east Africa's coastal area reserves. It is located a short drive south from the city of Mombasa and contains, in addition to lions, a large elephant population.

The following tour highlights those areas where a permanent lion population can be found and visitors can generally arrange to observe the animals from some amazingly close vantage points.

KENYA

Kenya offers the visitor the greatest number of parks and tourist facilities for visitors, with reserves offering many chances for close observations of lions.

Meru National Park

Meru National Park has a special place in the hearts of lion lovers because of its association with Joy and George Adamson and Elsa, the *Born Free* lion. Lying along the equator to the west of Mount Kenya, Meru contains 320 square miles (832 square kilometers) of mostly semiarid land. At one time in the 1950s, the big-game population had almost disappeared,

Most lions live in what is termed "scrub country". This is an area made up of grassy plains and thorny scrub trees. But lions have also been found living at 2-mile- (3.2-kilometre-) high altitudes on Mount Kenya.

Following page:

Two females are shown at rest in Kenya's Masai Mara Game Reserve. The long siestas taken by lions are often a means of cementing social connections.

This female lion is climbing a tree in Kenya's Masai Mara Game Reserve. Despite their great size and weight, lions can move among tree branches without even bending them.

The wind coming over the Masai Mara Game Reserve in Kenya ruffles the mane of this elderly male lion. A lion's mane gets darker as it grows older. These stately animals can live into their twenties.

Although the lion is not the most efficient predator in the animal kingdom, prey is so plentiful in most of the areas where lions now thrive that they are able to find enough food without much trouble.

This male lion takes a refreshing break at a Kenyan waterhole. The travels of a lion pride can be determined by the availability of water and prey during the dry season.

but conservation efforts turned this situation around.

This area is very remote and difficult for visitors to reach. It is therefore very unspoiled.

Kora National Reserve

Bordering Meru and running along the Tana River, the Kora National Reserve is where the Adamsons together, and later George Adamson with his associate Tony Fitzjohn, worked on various lion projects. George Adamson spent many years at the dangerous business of trying to reintroduce captured lions to the wild. Tragically, he was killed by bandits in 1988, but research work with lions and leopards continues at Adamson's Camp. This area is devoted to scientific research rather than tourism, but visits can be arranged and good views of the lions are available for those with time and patience.

Female lions stalk through the grass at the Masai Mara Game Reserve in Kenya. Lions generally pursue prey as a group effort and follow their intended kill for fifteen minutes to an hour before pouncing.

Masai Mara Game Reserve

The Masai Mara is made up of the Kenyan side of Tanzania's Serengeti, and is therefore part of one of the greatest wilderness and wildlife reserves in the world. This reserve contains many sizable lion prides.

The lions are supplied with abundant and replenished prey due to the yearly migration of millions of zebras, wildebeest, and other animals travelling from the dry grasslands of Tanzania to the south.

The huge, open spaces of the reserve, covering 720 square miles (1,872 square kilometres), provides wonderful views of the lion populace. Facilities for visitors are very good, and there is the opportunity for touring the reserve from a spectacular vantage point in hot-air balloons, silently floating above the African plain.

In the Masai Mara Game Reserve in Kenya, vultures circle overhead, biding their time as they watch a lioness preparing to make a kill. After the lions finish feeding on the carcass, the birds will feast on whatever remains.

Nairobi National Park

The Nairobi National Park is amazing for its very existence, located as it is just outside the city limits of Kenya's capital, Nairobi. One can leave the crowded, bustling streets of Nairobi and in twenty minutes be nearby a lion pride, or zebras, wildebeest, cheetahs, and other wildlife. The capital city's modern skyline, with high-rise office buildings and hotels, is actually visible from various points inside the park. In a single moment it is possible to witness an ages-old scene of lion's stalking prey while a jumbo jet aircraft crosses the horizon in the background.

Samburu National Reserve and Buffalo Springs National Reserve

These parks are in the dry, northern part of the country. The rugged, arid landscape means a mini-

Nairobi National Park is one of the most remarkable animal reserves in Africa, located as it is only 4 miles (6.4 kilometres) from the center of Kenya's capital city. One can actually see Nairobi's modern skyline from within the park.

This young lion is a resident of the Masai Mara Game Reserve in the east African nation of Kenya. Although it once thrived on several continents, the lion is now found almost exclusively in sub-Saharan Africa.

mum of covering vegetation, which gives the visitor clear views of the lion population. At the lodges here, it is often possible to see lions come very near to obtain bait.

Shimba Hills National Park

Shimba Hills is near the Kenyan coastline, 40 miles (64 kilometres) from the port city of Mombasa. The views through the rain forest along the coast are magnificent, but the small community of lions is found closer to the center of the park.

Tsavo (East and West) National Park

Encompassing 9,000 square miles (23,400 square kilometres), Tsavo National Park is a huge, rambling location with a variety of habitats, from marsh to mountains. Tsavo was once legendary for its huge elephant population and for the fact that the elephants were dyed red from the soil and dust in the park. Poachers have decimated the elephants over the past decade.

The lions of Tsavo are a relatively peaceful group compared to their relatives of a hundred years ago. At that time, the colonial government was building a railroad to Nairobi from Mombasa. The construction bogged down in Tsavo as countless railroad workers were attacked and eaten by the local big cats. The blood-curdling story was told in Colonel Patterson's *The Maneaters of Tsavo*, a bestseller in its day.

An early morning hunting party gathers in the Masai Mara Game Reserve in Kenya. The reserve, located along the Tanzanian border, is one of the best areas for observing lions and other big game.

Lions gather at the kill site in Tanzania. These animals do not kill in numbers that would affect the population growth of the prey in their habitat.

Accompanied by a cub, a lioness drags the carcass of a recent kill. Generally, a large kill means food for many lions at one time. The food is usually eaten quickly, rather than stored or guarded for future meals.

TANZANIA

Tanzania contains some of the most legendary wildlife reserves anywhere, from Serengeti and the fascinating Ngorongoro Crater, to Mount Kilimanjaro. In this region, lions roam over the sites of the earliest-known human fossil remains.

Lake Manyara National Park

Set along the Great Rift, Lake Manyara is a beautiful area of dramatic landscapes, with 130 square miles (338 square kilometres) of park land. Actually, most of that total is taken up by the lake itself, large portions of it covered by a million or more pink flamingos.

The lions here prove false the once widely held belief that lions do not climb trees. In fact, the Lake Manyara lions are often seen resting in acacia trees, whiling away their time until nightfall. The area is relatively unspoiled by human encroachment due to the prevalence of the tsetse fly.

A female lion stands beside the tall grasses of Ngorongoro Crater in Tanzania. Cut off from other areas by the walled-in crater, the lions are endangered by the increasing problem of inbreeding.

Lions like this one, a resident of Ngorongoro Crater in Tanzania, have been plagued by serious health hazards in recent years. A major problem has been the outbreak of tormenting, bloodsucking flies.

Mikumi National Park

An important area for wildlife researchers, Mikumi was made a national park in 1964, and is the third largest one in Tanzania.

The lions are most plentiful in the region north of the main road, along with herds of buffalo, hippopotamuses, elephants, zebras, and leopards. The lions here have gotten used to the presence of humans and vehicles in the area.

Ngorongoro Crater

Although it makes up only a small portion of the conservation area, the Ngorongoro Crater is the main attraction here. A crater within an extinct volcano, its 100-square-mile (260-square-

These animals are residents of the Ngorongoro Crater in Tanzania. The 100-square-mile (260-square-kilometre) floor of the crater is home to six separate lion prides. Naturalists have named each pride after aspects of the crater.

With their very strong limbs, lions can spring a great distance into the air—sometimes jumping into the boughs of trees.

kilometre) floor is home to six separate lion prides. Naturalists have named each pride after aspects of the crater.

The Ngorongoro Crater is in effect an island, cut off from the surrounding area. This isolation has had its good and bad points. The crater has one of the most congested wildlife populations in Africa, making the lions' search for prey quite easy. On the other hand, the islandlike setting has kept out newcomers and fresh genetic strains, leading to dangerous inbreeding. Over one hundred lions reside in the crater, while three thousand lions live in the Ngorongoro beyond the crater.

Ruaha National Park

Although it is Tanzania's second-largest game reserve, Ruaha is also remote and difficult to reach, and parts of it are completely cut off in the rainy season. Several lion prides can be found in the scrub and grassland areas of the park.

Serengeti National Park

The Serengeti National Park contains the greatest numbers of African big game anywhere on the continent. Serengeti stretches across nearly 6,000 square miles (15,600 square kilometres) of hills and plains. Vast herds of wildebeest, buffalo, gazelles, zebras, and others are spread across the area. The lion population enjoys such an abundance of prey that the prides seldom need to go outside their range.

The government has maintained the Serengeti without any of the more gimmicky tourist facilities and attractions offered at other reserves, thus making it the most unspoiled of all the great national parks in east Africa.

The lions of the Lake Manyara area of Tanzania are known for their tree climbing—and tree sitting. Some spend entire days perched in a comfortable tree branch.

This young male lion is a resident of South Africa's Kalahari Gemsbok. In this sanctioned habitat, the lion population thrives. Other reserves have not fared as well.

An African lion drinks from a waterhole in the Kalahari Gemsbok in South Africa. Dimly visible in the background is an approaching blue wildebeest.

SOUTH AFRICA

Colonialism in southern Africa in the early nineteenth century led to the extinction of at least one regional subspecies, the Cape lion, the last of which expired in the 1860s. Despite this loss, there are still other noteworthy lion-watching sites.

Kruger National Park

South Africa's largest game reserve is the last home of the Transvaal lion, a subspecies that was indigenous to the southeast tip of the continent.

Kalahari Gemsbok

The smaller of South Africa's main lion reserves, the stark landscape of the Kalahari allows for many unobstructed views of the big cats going about their daily lives.

OTHER AFRICAN COUNTRIES

Though not as well known as some of the other African wildlife parks, the following make for interesting lion-watching experiences.

Uganda: Queen Elizabeth National Park

Though threatened by civil war and other internal upheaval, this country has taken great care to nurture its massive wildlife population. In some places, however, poaching and neglect have definitely taken their toll.

Queen Elizabeth National Park is Uganda's greatest game reserve. Set against the Ruwenzori Mountains, it is a rich and beautiful region with a varied topography. For lion watchers, the place to go is the southern section of the park, called Ishasha. Difficult to reach at times, Ishasha is considered one of the most unspoiled game-viewing areas in Africa.

What distinguishes the lions in this 30-square-mile (78-square-kilometer) section is their propensity for climbing and resting in the local fig trees. It is not unusual to come upon a tree with two or three lions lazily perched in its boughs—a startling sight, and one seen on a regular basis only at one other game reserve, Lake Manyara in Tanzania. It is not certain exactly why the lions of Queen Elizabeth indulge in this habit. Some believe it is to escape the biting flies, which can be a major nuisance on the ground.

Ethiopia: Bale Mountains National Park

As in Uganda, political and social upheavals have threatened the wildlife preservation efforts in Ethiopia. Being a low priority on the government's agenda, the country's animals reserves are difficult to reach but well worth the effort.

The Bale Mountains National Park is Ethiopia's most important wildlife reserve, with a great variety of species and habitat. For viewing lions, one heads for the grasslands at Katcha. Few tourists come here, compared to the hordes that sometimes seem to turn the popular parks in Kenya into large-scale zoos. Visitors here are able to observe the lion populace under almost pristine, natural circumstances.

With sundown
approaching, a
grown male lion
lies in repose
in South Africa's
Kalahari Gems-
bok. Lions in the
wild are now
found chiefly in
Africa's regulated
game parks.

Following page:

The noble lion
is pictured in a
characteristic
sphinx-type pose,
photographed
near sunset in
Kalahari Gemsbok,
a lion reserve
in South Africa
open to visitors.

Almost all remaining subspecies of lions are now African. Early in the twentieth century, the Indian lion population was down to barely more than a dozen. After being placed under protection by the government, there are now approximately 250 lions in India.

Rwanda: Akagera National Park

Rwanda is a densely populated, mountainous central-eastern African nation. This small country is better known for its mountain gorillas than its lion population. And, in fact, the lions of Akagera are not as reliable "performers" as those in the famed east African reserves, but Rwanda's lush setting makes the trip worth the effort.

INDIA

Gir National Park and Lion Sanctuary

Far removed from their African cousins, the lions of Gir are the only remaining colony of Indian, or Asiatic, lions. Even this enclave came very close to being wiped out and continues to have a questionable future due to the encroachments of humans and herds of grazing cattle, which force out the lion's natural prey.

The Gir population now stands at around 250. But visitors will find them far from elusive. The Gir lions have learned to live with the presence of humans and automobiles, so that close viewings by visitors are almost certain.

The park is closed during the monsoon season, and the best months for visiting are between December and May.

Although the lion survives in limited numbers in India today, it does retain a place of importance there. In fact, the lion is the emblem of the Republic of India.

Here is a rare glimpse of an Indian lioness, whose existence is now limited to a protected area of the Gir Forest in Kathiawar. The Indian lion was once threatened with complete extinction.

The Asiatic, or Indian, lion is smaller than the African version. Indian male lions also tend to have a more close-cropped mane. Despite their more diminutive stature, Indian lions are still quite mighty and magnificent animals.

Although they are now small in number, Asiatic lions have long been an important symbol in the Indian culture. The lion, known as the Lord of Beasts in Indian myth, was continually depicted as a symbol of strength and sovereignty.

At one time, the Indian lion could be found in a wide area across the northern part of the subcontinent. Today the 116 square miles (302 square kilometres) of Gir National Park and Lion Sanctuary is the only remaining home for the Asiatic animal.

THE FUTURE OF THE LION

The lion is here to stay—at least for the foreseeable future. Unlike so many other animals in this century, lions are not among those listed on any endangered species list, and none of the major remaining lion populations face any immediate threat of extinction. This is good news to be sure, although the idea that we can feel grateful that a creature has not been entirely wiped out indicates a woeful state of affairs in the natural world.

Parks, Reserves, and Wildlife Organisations

As it is, the wave of global interest in ecology, conservation, and wildlife protection that began to take hold in the 1960s came soon enough to give the African lion a new lease on life. Newly independent governments confronted two related facts: that tourism was a major or potentially major source of income for countries with large wildlife populations and, second, that the same wildlife was seriously in danger of being wiped out from hunting, poaching, and habitat encroachment. A nation anxious for income from tourism could no sooner afford to lose its lions than Miami, Florida, could afford to lose its beaches. The system of national parks and reserves began to develop, with game wardens and, where necessary, armed militia to protect the animals.

Other organisations, governmental and otherwise, including a number of nonprofit international groups—such as the African Wildlife Foundation, the Elsa Wild Animal Appeal, Wildlife Conservation International, the East African Wild Life Society, and the Worldwide Fund

A lion pride's territory and population can only expand if certain criteria are met. There must be enough game and water, as well as sufficient numbers of shady resting spots.

Several lion breeds survive today. The Masai lion lives in some of the protected areas of east Africa. The Senegalese lion lives in west Africa, along with other regional subspecies, including the Angolan, Rhodesian, and Transvaal lions.

for Nature—are among other organisations with programs specifically aimed at aiding Africa's healthy but limited population of wild lions thrive in the century to come.

One Possible Future

But the lion's "safety net" in the wild is not indestructible, and the future still holds pitfalls for this remarkable creature. The killings and habitat destruction of the past continue to affect the "protected" lion population of the present. The balance of nature is delicate, and once upset is not easy to set right again. When wilderness areas become fragmented, cut apart by human encroachment, the already-thinned lion populations become isolated. The number of potential mating pairs becomes smaller and the gene pool more limited. The long-term effects of inbreeding are an

A protected area for wildlife since 1948, Amboseli National Park was one of the first game reserves established in east Africa. Amboseli's open landscapes give visitors remarkable, unimpeded views of its lion population.

While now confined to Africa and a tiny area in India, lions were once plentiful in the Middle East and Greece.

This young adult is stalking its prey up a tree. Like other members of the cat family, the lion is a great leaper. There are reports of lions leaping as far as a spectacular 40 feet (12.1 metres).

The lion is one of the larger members of the cat family. It is distantly related to Felis catus, better known as the domestic cat, and shares many of the same characteristics of appearance and behavior.

Lions were once native to many parts of Europe, according to such evidence as cave paintings found in France. However, with the exception of Greece, they have not been found in the European wild since recorded history.

A lion in Botswana charges the photographer of this picture. Some tourists to Africa, apparently confusing game parks with zoos, take lethal risks in the presence of wild animals. Some tourists are attacked and a few killed by lions every year.

Once prevalent in ancient Greece, lions were described by Aristotle as scarce by 300 B.C. By A.D. 100 there were no further reported sightings of lions in Greece.

The lion's scientific name is Panthera leo. It is sandy brown in colour and is found in Africa and in India. Its closest relatives are the other majestic big cats: the tiger, the jaguar, and the leopard.

increase in congenital defects, infertility, and a weakened immune system. When this occurs, a lion population—no matter how well protected within the boundaries of a national park—begins to shrink and deteriorate. It is a downward spiral that can mean the end of isolated lion groups, despite the best efforts of a government to hold off destructive acts.

The best test case for this potential "genetic erosion" in many lion reserves was observed in the Ngorongoro Crater in Tanzania. Animal biologist Craig Packer and his associate and wife, Ann Pusey, made a long-range study of the Ngorongoro's six lion prides, animals in a sense "marooned" on the 100-square-mile (260-square-kilometre) floor of the crater.

Their findings are that the isolated environment has fostered a series of circumstances leading to continued inbreeding. Through research and inspired detective work, Packer found that the Ngorongoro lions had gone through a number of cycles of reduced breeding population followed by genetic decline. First, hunters in the 1920s killed off a large percentage of adult males in a short span of time. Thereafter, a plague of bloodsucking flies reduced the lion populace to a handful in the early 1960s—the lions' susceptibility to the flies perhaps already indicated an immune deficiency from inbreeding.

Packer's research showed that the current population of one hundred or so lions in Ngorongoro are all descendants of just fifteen animals in the crater, and that the past five generations of lions were the products of close inbreeding. The crater lions were found to have lost considerable genetic diversity, having only half that of the less isolated Serengeti lions. Their reproductive rates were down, and they showed weakened immune systems. The potential for grave long-term effects on the crater lions may be a harbinger for the future of other lion populations locked within the boundaries of some animal reserves.

A more direct menace than inbreeding is the continued hunting and trapping of the African lion. Of the two east African nations with the greatest lion populations, Kenya continues to uphold a complete ban on lion hunting, but the government of Tanzania rescinded its ban in the 1980s, in order to increase revenues from foreign sport hunters. Difficult as it may be to believe, there are still people in the world willing to pay lots of money for the "privilege" of pointlessly shooting and killing a wild lion.

In addition to the animals lost to sport hunting, many lions are killed by poachers, mostly local tribesmen trying to trap animals for meat. The lions are inadvertently caught in the traps in these cases. Others trap and kill lions in order to sell body parts. Among some African tribes, the lion's claws and teeth are considered good luck talismans, while certain internal organs are thought to provide special powers when consumed.

This young male is ready for a catnap, using an uncomfortable-looking tree trunk as a pillow. Lions are often inactive, resting or sleeping for as much as twenty hours per day.

Following page:

Although lions are not slow compared to other animals in general, they are not as fast as many other predators competing for food in their habitat. The maximum speed of a lion is about 30 miles (48 kilometres) per hour.

A young African male lion yawns luxuriously. No matter how carefully the world's zoos try to simulate a natural environment, only in the wild can the lion experience the full range of its intended existence.

In a German zoo, a pair of lions was observed mating more than three hundred times in a one-week period.

Zoos

Once, not too long ago, zoos were considered nothing more than permanent exhibits, offering patrons a vivid glimpse of the exotic and dangerous creatures of the world's wilderness regions. Today, a zoo can be a scientific lab, a breeding center, and last refuge for endangered species no longer welcome in their homeland. In the past a zoo seeking to add a new lion to its collection would send for one to be captured and shipped from the wild. This is no longer feasible for various reasons, and so zoos have to create self-sustaining captive populations. Lions have bred very well in captivity, and all major and most minor zoos have them on exhibit.

Zoos have progressed greatly from bygone years, when animals were held in small, cramped cages. Today, zoos often create elaborate ambient enclosures, evoking the wilderness the animals came from with thick growths of vegetation, rocks, and waterholes. Nowadays as much attention is paid to the animals' psychological needs as to their physical needs.

Zoos attempt to create spaces with many visual barriers, giving the cats a chance to separate and not be face to face with each other at all times. Although lions do not hunt for their food in zoos, they are fed a raw, red meat diet similar to what they would devour in the wild, with the male being given slightly more than the female, as would occur in nature.

In the wild, the rigours of survival and the recurring necessity for hunting and catching prey keeps the lion's instincts sharp and mind alert. The captive lion can easily become bored and depressed from the lack of challenge, so zoos have to find ways of reactivating the cats' instincts and abilities. One effective method for accomplishing this is so-called environmental enrichment, in which new elements are brought into an enclosure and new challenges offered the lions. Keepers do what is known as "logpiling", in which food treats are hidden under piles of logs so that the cats must work to discover and then find them. Some zoos offer the lions "boomer balls", heavy-duty plastic balls containing similar treats inside. The balls are sometimes floated in pools of water—since the lions do not enjoy swimming, it means considerable mental concentration and physical effort to try and retrieve the balls without getting too wet. "You would be surprised how much good these little games can do", says Craig Lewis, Senior Keeper at Washington Park Zoo in Oregon. "The challenge is very exciting for the lions. Something new, something to break up the day periodically, is as important to a lion's mental health and alertness as it is to a human's".

Zookeepers and animal researchers continually work to find new ways of challenging their captive population. Lions are traditionally one of the most popular attractions at any major zoo, but exhibiting is only one of the things zoos do with their resident lions. The breeding of lions, whether for captive propagation programs, or for the future necessity of reintroduction into the wild, presents special challenges for zoos. The bloodlines and genetic backgrounds of many captive lions are very tangled. As researcher Dr. Jill Mellen explains, "In the old days, it was not considered impor-

This beautiful cat displays its mighty paw. A lion's paws are extremely powerful, with very sharp, retractable claws.

tant to keep records about the origins of particular lions. Asian lions were bred with African lions and so on. But for reintroduction to the wild, it would be inappropriate to put an Asian lion, say, into the African wild, or a lion of South African origin into east Africa". Zoos are now attempting to separate lions for breeding by assigned sub-species, under the assumption that a lion bred for a particular environment is most likely to thrive in that same environment.

But at the same time, they are conducting genetic research on lions to determine what exactly are the genetic differences.

Through the centuries, mankind has done much to honour the lion's existence and much to threaten it. We must hope that the future interaction of lion and man will emphasize the honour, and put an end to the threats.

During the dry season in east Africa, lion prides become concentrated along stretches of river. Though the prides often overlap, this usually does not present a serious problem.

The Barbary lion, one of several subspecies now considered extinct, could once be found from Morocco to Egypt. The last pure Barbary was shot in Morocco in 1920.

INDEX OF PHOTOGRAPHERS

SPIDER

The story of a predator and its prey

written and photographed by
Dick Jones

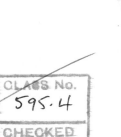
ORBIS · LONDON

The publishers would like to thank the following organisations and individuals for their permission to reproduce the additional photographs in this book:

Anthony Bannister/NHPA 45 below left; James Carmichael Jnr/NHPA 28; Stephen Dalton/NHPA 45 top; Adrian Davies/ Bruce Coleman Ltd 46/47; Mary Evans Picture Library 6, 8 (©Barbara Edwards); Sonia Halliday and Laura Lushington 7 left; K.G. Preston-Mafham/Premaphotos Wildlife 16; John Shaw/ Bruce Coleman Ltd 26

Orb web artwork by Richard Lewington/The Garden Studio All other line drawings by Christopher Shields

Illustration right: a doomed grasshopper has fallen foul of *Agelena labyrinthica's* large and complex sheet web

First published in Great Britain 1986 by
Orbis Book Publishing Corporation Ltd

A BPCC plc company

©Orbis Book Publishing Corporation Ltd 1986

Printed in Singapore
ISBN 1-85515-007-0

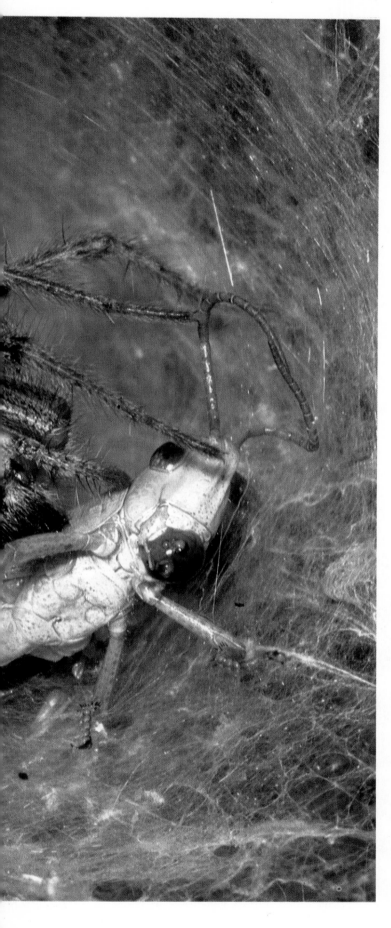

CONTENTS

INTRODUCTION

'The skin of it is so soft, smooth, polished and neat, that she precedes the softest skin'd Mayds, and the daintiest and most beautiful Strumpets, and is so clear that you may almost see your face in her as in a glasse; she hath fingers that the most gallant Virgins desire to have theirs like them, long, slender, round, of exact feeling, that there is no man, nor any creature that can compare with her.'

Dr Thomas Mouffet 1553–1604

In the days when the ancient Greek gods lived on Mount Olympus, a maiden named Arachne, boastful of her skill in weaving, challenged the goddess Athene to a contest to decide which of them was the more accomplished weaver. Athene accepted the challenge and the contestants began work at their looms. When at last they had finished, they turned to look at each other's work. Arachne's tapestry was exceedingly fine, but when she saw the efforts of the goddess, she realised she was beaten. Shattered by the blow of losing the contest after all her boasting, Arachne tried to hang herself. But Athene would not be satisfied by the mere death of her rival, and condemned her to an eternity of spinning and weaving; Arachne was transformed into a spider.

An ancient line

This myth, ingenious though it is, tells us little about the origin of spiders and how they developed their wonderful ability to spin silk. It would seem likely that they evolved from aquatic species

During the mediaeval period, the distinctive markings on A. diadematus (the garden spider) were thought to represent the sign of the cross

Above: *an early 19th century engraving portraying the downfall of Arachne; her arrogance has caused her to be turned into a spider*

at the very dawn of life on dry land, emerging from the primeval oceans along with scorpions (like spiders, members of the class Arachnida) and millipedes. Scorpions appear to be descended from the extinct eurypterids (sea scorpions), which resemble giant lobsters, but the ancestry of spiders remains a mystery, like their development in geological times; the fossil record they have left us is maddeningly incomplete since throughout the long ages our world has endured, few spiders have been fossilised, but it is interesting to note that many of these are familiar in their membership of families we recognise now, and in at least one instance they are virtually indistinguishable from the modern species.

The genus *Homo*, to which we belong, emerged in the relatively recent past, about 5 million years ago, but not until 40,000 year ago did modern man appear – 400 million years behind the spiders! Primitive man was more conscious of his place in nature than we are, and although spiders probably had little direct effect on the lives of our hunting ancestors, their enviable predatory skills were not overlooked.

Weavers of legend

The faint silhouette of a spider surrounded by dead flies adorns the wall of a prehistoric site in a Spanish cave, while on the Nazca Plain in Peru there is a huge outline drawing of a spider amongst the many other mysterious images that can be seen only from the air. On every continent there are spider legends based on close observation of their web-making skills or predatory activities; in many of these, a spider becomes the benefactor of man by teaching him the techniques of basket-making and weaving. Others, however, attributed a villainous role to the spider, in which it took on human form and lured people to their deaths.

Since Roman times spiders have been valued for their supposed power to prevent or cure a bewildering variety of ailments, and they were often worn as a living charm encased in a suitable package and hung around the sufferer's neck. In spite of an admonition at the end of the sixteenth century that these 'foolish toies' were of no use, medical science later intensified its support of the creature and patients were advised to swallow the unfortunate spider, not just wear it; in 1760, one Dr Watson advised that a fever could be cured by 'swallowing a spider gently bruised and wrapped up in a raisin or spread upon bread and butter'.

Spinning and leaping

Meanwhile, in southern Italy, a large wolf spider known as a tarantula (after the port of Taranto) was making its presence felt, and from the fifteenth to the seventeenth centuries a great many peasants were said to have fallen victim to this persistent predator, whose bite resulted in the victim crying, leaping about uncontrollably and launching into a frenetic dance. Whether this performance was a symptom brought on by the poison, or an attempt to purge the body of it is not clear, but in any case the creature lent its name to a lively folk dance in six-eight time, the Tarantella. Confusingly, the term tarantula does not denote a particular spider, but is applied to many large tropical ones, irrespective of their natural affinities.

The writing on the web

A common country belief is that the presence of filmy threads in the grass foretells clear and calm

Above: *this charmingly painted scene of a spider in peril from a hungry robin is featured on a 15th century glass panel in York Minster*

Above: *our ancestors believed the appearance of fine silvery threads in the grass to be the result of a powerful magic force at work*

weather conditions, but this theory rather puts the cart before the horse; in fact it is only on warm still days, particularly in the autumn, that this material is dispersed.

When warm air currents are rising from the ground, the spiders climb up to elevated positions on blades of grass or twigs and emit long strands of silk from their abdomens. When the lines are long enough to catch this movement of air, the little creatures are borne aloft: this aerial travel is known as 'ballooning'. Very often the spider's journey is quite short, the silken line soon becoming entangled in nearby vegetation, but some spiders have been seen several miles up and others have landed on ships far out at sea.

In particularly good years, millions of tiny spiders are carried through the air each day, and when dusk comes and condensation forms on their lines, they drift slowly down to earth. As soon as they land, still on their lines, they build

their little individual webs of similar material, and the next morning vast tracts of ground are covered in glistening silk. To people in former times, this had the appearance of the goose down commonly seen in late summer when geese were killed and plucked. The time of year – and the substance – became known as 'goose-summer', or gossamer.

Most of the small, black spiders who carry on this aerial dispersal belong to the large *Linyphiidae* family, popularly and collectively known as 'money' spiders. The superstitions associated with finding one of these small creatures on one's person are wide ranging: some believe they are simply bringers of good luck, while others associate them with a gift of new clothes (woven by the spider perhaps) or the acquisition of gold or cash.

Spidermania
Mankind in general has contradictory feelings toward spiders, unwarrantedly attributing good

Above: *since her father, the 16th century physician Thomas Mouffet, believed that spiders had healing properties when eaten, it is not surprising that 'Little Miss Muffet' was distressed at the mere sight of such a creature*

luck to their presence at one moment; in the next, fearing them irrationally. Even in today's aseptic world, when spiders may be feared even more than they were in the past because they are less familiar, most people feel superstitious reluctance to kill one, and will attempt to remove it instead. In the case of some unfortunate individuals, an overpowering and irrational terror of spiders – arachnophobia – rules their lives.

This condition is extremely well-known, although it affects very few people. Indeed, research indicates that more people are afraid of snakes than of spiders; the difference is that snakes are seldom in evidence (except on television), while spiders are a common sight, since we provide shelter for them in our homes, and our food attracts the insects they feed on.

Not all spiders are so enamoured of Man that

they wish to live with him – a few steps into the countryside will reveal a wealth of delicate and prettily marked species – but it is one of the many ironies about spiders that the largest, hairiest and most evil-looking are found in and around the house. Unfortunately, among the several species of house spider are those with the greatest leg span, and this is often cited as particularly abhorrent, but most domestic pets have longer, hairier legs and in humans, long legs are deemed attractive.

We don't seem to be so alarmed by cobwebs, but when their builders are caught in our living rooms, that is a different matter. This doesn't happen any more often than the spider can help; most live in their webs, where they will remain contentedly if they are catching the odd titbit, and they can go for considerable periods without food or drink. But if they have not caught anything and are getting hungry, they must move to a new and perhaps better site. It is on these excursions that they tend to be seen, although increased sightings in the autumn may be due to movement by males in search of females. So it is either food or sex that drives them out of the security of their webs into a dangerous and often unsympathetic world. These spiders are desperately vulnerable out of their webs, and when caught out in the open, clinging ludicrously to the walls or strolling across the carpet, they have only two options for staying alive: to remain perfectly still and hope they won't be noticed, or to run as fast as their legs will carry them. They are practically blind, and so can just as easily run towards you as away in their efforts to escape. In fact, the poor creature's fear of man is wholly justified, while our horror and distrust of it constitutes a great injustice. The spider not only does not eat our food; it is a major predator of the insects who do, and since no spider has ever been implicated in spreading disease, they are much less dangerous than even a house fly, which scares nobody.

Labels and fables

When we come to discuss the various types of spiders, we find it necessary to employ Latin names to avoid confusion since, like many creatures, spiders often have no common name or numerous local ones. In the eighteenth century, scientists realised that it would be convenient to ensure that everybody used the same name for each animal or plant and the Swedish scientist Linnaeus devised a system using the classical languages of Greek and Latin with which educated people of all nationalities were familiar. Each organism was given two names, a sort of first name (species) and surname (genus), but in the scientific notation, the 'surname' comes first. If, for example, we take the common European house spider, we find that there are three main species: *Tegenaria gigantea*, *T. domestica* and *T. parietina*. (Note that the scientific names are always printed in italics, and that members of the same genus have their 'surname' abbreviated after the first citation.) The use of the one English name 'house spider' is particularly confusing here, since there are three distinct species. To add to this confusion, the number of species known as house spiders starts multiplying as soon as we leave the confines of one country and go to another. In America, only two of the three English *Tegenaria* species are found, along with the further species *Achaearanea tepidariorum* and *Oecobius annulipes*, both of which are very widespread in warm climates, being found in Australian homes too. Because of the constant traffic between different parts of the world spiders are freely exchanged, although as far as we can tell, the majority of these eight-legged jet-setters originate from Europe. They all might be known as 'house' spiders, yet the three genera mentioned above differ greatly from each other in shape, size and web form. In short, there is no universal house spider, although one of the globe-trotting *Tegenarias* might well take the title eventually.

The identification of the genus and species to which a spider, and any other creature, belongs is part of the scheme that scientists have devised to classify all living things. Naturalists recognise that many animals (and plants) have certain characteristics in common and they have used these to place them also in broader groups than the genus/species we have been looking at. Collections of genera with similar features are known as *families*, and this applies to spiders as much as to other creatures. (We have already seen that money spiders, for example, all belong to the *Linyphiidae* family.) All spiders together form a vast group known as an order, which is divided into three sub-orders that contain the various families. The two most important of these sub-groups are the *Mygalomorphae* and the *Araneomorphae* (the third sub-order – the *Mesothelae* – contains only nine species), and these divisions are based on the way the spiders' fangs move. The mygalomorph's fangs (A) are vertically placed and parallel to each other, so the spider must rear up to attack its victim with a forward, thrusting movement. The fangs of the

araneomorphs (B) however, are placed in a line, facing each other horizontally, and are able to open and close, catching prey between them.

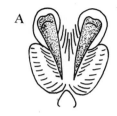
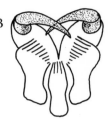

Above: *the wider span of araneomorph spiders' opposed fangs makes it possible for them to overpower large prey*

The *Mygalomorphae* take their name from the Greek words for 'like a field-mouse' from a fancied resemblance to that animal. Some large and imposing species of this group (most commonly the southern American *Brachypelma smithi* or, more colourfully, Mexican Red Knee), are sold in pet shops under the names of 'bird-eating spiders' or 'tarantulas'. Since they mostly eat insects and the name *Tarantula* applies to other sorts of spider as we have seen, neither of the common names is really correct and the term mygalomorph, though not exactly descriptive, is at least universally understood to refer to the same group of spiders.

The *Araneomorphae* are the so-called 'true spiders' and included in this group are the spiders known popularly as the orb web weavers. Whilst they share many physical characteristics, not all of them actually weave webs, so we can see that this common name is inadequate too, whereas the scientific name of the group – *Araneidae* – labels these animals with complete accuracy.

It is easy to see from these examples how misleading the use of popular names in natural history can be, and in fact there is such an enormous number of spider species that most do not even have common names and can only be identified by the scientific terms. This huge range of species is matched by the fascinating variations in behaviour that spiders exhibit and that become obvious on closer examination – as you will see when you read of their exploits in the following pages.

FORM AND FUNCTION

'To praise the spider as I ought, I shall first set before you the riches of its body, then of its fortune, lastly of its minde.'

Thomas Mouffet in *Theatrum Insectorum*, 1634

Spiders are not insects – on the contrary they are one of the most important predators of these creatures, which include some of Man's most dangerous adversaries. Spiders are measured by the length of their bodies; the spread of their legs is excluded although it is this that makes them appear much bigger than they really are. The smallest adult spider known is only half a millimetre long, but most spiders measure between 5 and 10mm and the European house spider, despite some descriptions I have heard, is a mere 18mm in body length. In reality, the largest spider known is the hairy South American mygalomorph *Theraphosa leblondii*, a monster with a body 90mm long and a leg span of 280mm – sufficient to cover a dinner plate!

Lethal liquids

Unlike most creatures familiar to us, which must swallow their food and digest it internally, spiders are incapable of swallowing solid particles and consequently have small and inconspicuous

Typical of the jumping spiders, Aelurillus cervinus *has large, forward-directed eyes that give clear focus and accurate colour vision*

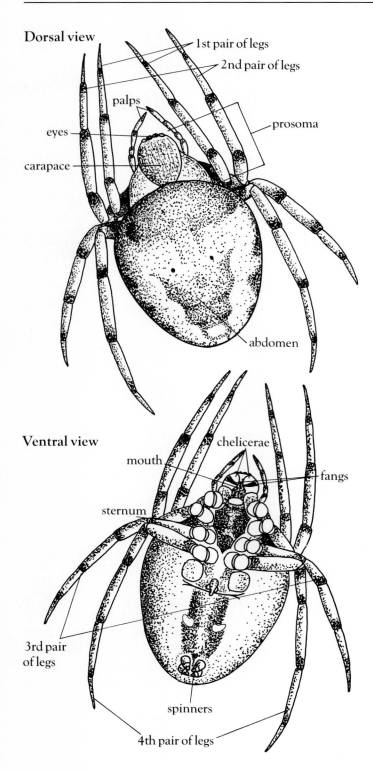

Dorsal view

1st pair of legs
2nd pair of legs
palps
eyes
carapace
prosoma
abdomen

Ventral view

mouth
chelicerae
sternum
fangs
3rd pair of legs
spinners
4th pair of legs

This highly stylised drawing sets out the anatomy of a spider. While the posterior section, the abdomen, is soft, the front portion, the prosoma, is protected by two horny plates, the carapace on top and the sternum underneath. Digestion, circulation, respiration, reproduction and silk production are carried on from the abdomen; locomotion and feeding from the prosoma

mouth parts. The prey is first held in the spider's *chelicerae* (jaws) and punctured by the fangs, which inject a poison.

The chemical composition of spider venom varies considerably from species to species; in a very few kinds there is no poison at all. The infamous black widow spider is armed with a poison that can be lethal or merely unpleasant to human beings, depending on their age, health and size, but out of thirty or forty thousand species of spider only about twenty are dangerous to man.

Once the poison has been injected into the prey, digestive liquids are released over it. When these have liquefied the softer parts of the prey, the resulting 'soup' is ingested by means of the sucking stomach. Some spiders have the base of the chelicerae furnished with teeth that enable them to crush their prey into an unrecognizable mess, but those spiders without these teeth leave their meals in a perfect state of preservation, except, of course, that they are empty husks. Some spiders cannot open their chelicerae very wide, and even with their normal prey, which is small, they can only bite it on an appendage, such as a leg or a wing.

The spider's abdomen is the equivalent of the mammal's trunk, containing the heart, lungs and intestinal tract. In addition, at the posterior end are the characteristic organs of spiders, the three pairs of spinners. The abdomen is covered, like the joints of the limbs, in a soft and elastic cuticle, which in a starved spider can be quite wrinkled, but which after drinking or feeding becomes bloated. Spiders have a low metabolic rate that enables them to go without food for long periods if necessary. Some species of *Steatoda*, for example, are extraordinary survivors: John Blackwell, the famous British arachnologist, kept a *Steatoda bipunctata* in 'a phial which was closely corked and locked up in a book-case . . . from the 15th of October 1829 to the 30th of April 1831, when it died'. This spider endured a fast of eighteen and a half months, and I myself have kept an individual of the same species in a small tube with a completely airtight polythene stopper and an internal volume of about 4cc. After a year I released the spider, none the worse for its deprivations, into my garden. It had survived without food or water and with only about two thimblefuls of air during its confinement.

The hunter and its prey
This ability to survive fasts and the rapacious manner in which spiders attack prey, especially

if they are very hungry, tells us something about their hunting prowess: however clever they may appear in catching, for example, flies, spiders are in fact very inefficient predators. The web weavers do not actively catch their prey – the prey catches itself, rather like a fish caught in a net. Hunting spiders, particularly the nocturnal kinds, do little *real* hunting: if luck permits them to come within striking distance of a potential prey, their senses will inform them of its whereabouts and they will pounce. If they wander all night without coming close to anything tasty then there are plenty more nights in which to have a meal, but the spider that cannot grasp the opportunity to feed when it *does* present itself will not last very long – it will either die of starvation or gradually become weakened and fall prey to one of its fellows or a predatory insect.

Orb-weaving spiders must be similarly speedy in reaching their prey for the web will not hold powerful, struggling insects indefinitely. There is, however, one group of spiders that have no need to hurry in coming to grips with their prey, and do not fear even pompilid wasps, the mortal enemies of most spiders – this group is known as the *cribellates*. Cribellate spiders have an additional

Above: *some spiders like this* Steatoda bipunctata *can survive for over a year between meals, and even shorter-lived ones endure extraordinary fasts; a small wolf spider with a life span of under a year can go 200 days without food*

Above: *the cribellate spider* Amaurobius similis *has on its rear legs a row of bristles covered with tiny cuticular teeth that comb out the silk. Because of its fine structure, cribellate silk can snare any insect unlucky enough to come into contact with it*

Above: *each jumping species has a unique pattern of facial hair, which is often more pronounced in the male, as with* Evarcha arcuata

spinning organ (the cribellum) from which very fine silk can issue, and whereas the threads of ecribellate species (those without the cribellum) are about 1μm in diameter (one twenty-five thousandth of an inch), the cribellate thread is at least a hundred times finer and therefore more efficient in entangling prey.

Close families
Because all spiders are predatory and will readily prey on other spiders as well as insects, it is surprising to find that one or two weaving species live socially, at least for a time. Newly-hatched spiderlings living in very close proximity to each other for various lengths of time are usually at a stage where the predatory habit has not yet developed, and are still subsisting on the remains of the egg yolk within them. A few species feed their young whilst they remain 'at home' so it can

be assumed that they can differentiate between food and family at this early stage. However, once they take up their solitary lives as hunters and weavers, family ties are well and truly broken and they will eat each other.

There are various mechanisms among the hunting spiders that prevent too much cannibalism within the species. Individuals that have grown large hunt in places where larger prey is to be found; the young ones usually occupy a different stratum of the habitat (often nearer the ground), where they are removed from the attentions of the larger spiders, and yet where they can find the small prey they can easily deal with.

Adult males have a shorter span of life than females. This is long enough for them to mate but most males die before the female lays her eggs, removing any competition between them for food and allowing the females to fatten up and so lay more eggs. Although there is a widely-held belief that, with spiders, the wedding breakfast consists of the groom (and certainly it is not unknown for the female to devour her mate) more often the

happy couple enjoy a relationship not found in many of the so-called higher animals.

In a number of species, including the European house spider, the male co-exists quite peacefully with his mate; a week or two after mating, he becomes gradually more lethargic and, his role in life completed, dies – then the female may scavenge on his remains. This may sound gruesome to us, but for the female spider it would be a waste of protein to let the corpse go uneaten – a simple case of waste not, want not.

Lenses and other senses

Most spiders have eight eyes, but some have six, four, or even one (an oddity found in the jungles of Panama). One Hawaiian species (*Adelocosa anops*), of a genus normally remarkable for the large size of the eyes, has no eyes at all and as a result has been given a comically contradictory common name – no-eyed, big-eyed wolf spider. Most of the day-active hunting spiders have reasonably good vision, at least at close quarters, and one orb-weaving spider, *Dinopis*, has eyes that are so big

Above: the body of a spider is covered in hairs; some are short and fine while others, like those on this Avicularia, *give a furry effect*

they pass more light to the retina than in any other animal, enabling it to detect movement even at night. It may seem perverse, however, that the majority of eight-eyed species appear to be all but blind, perhaps being able to distinguish little more than day from night. But spiders are literally bristling with an array of other sensory devices for the capture of prey and the avoidance of predators, so it is not surprising that some have abandoned sight in favour of their tactile senses.

Spiders have hairs, spines and bristles known collectively as *setae* (singular *seta*) that are often difficult to distinguish from each other. A few spiders have very short, fine setae and appear almost hairless, but others are quite furry with hairs of different colours making up a pattern. All the setae have sensory functions and are connected to the animal's brain, giving information on the proximity and nature of its prey.

Above: *their highly articulated limbs make spiders well-constructed to manipulate prey. This hapless moth is being devoured by a crab spider*

Spiders are well known for their long hairy legs, and it is on these that the most sensitive setae are to be found. At the ends of the legs and *palps* (leg-like appendages) there are numerous hairs that have hollow tips and are sensitive to chemical substances, endowing the animal with what has been called a 'touch-taste' sense. An orb web spider may have more than a thousand of these chemo-sensitive hairs concentrated on the last segment of each leg. As soon as the prey is touched it can be assessed as being palatable or not; at the same time its size can be estimated – most hunting spiders will not tackle prey larger than themselves, although there are some notable exceptions to this: the male crab spider *Thomisus* is only 3mm long, yet it has even been known to ambush bees.

Spiders also have extremely fine hairs, known as *trichobothria*, set in sockets with a flexible membrane that allows the hairs to waft with the faintest disturbance of the air, such as might be caused by the movement of prey.

Versatile legs

The flexibility of the legs is demonstrated by the ability of the weaving spiders, when knocked out of their webs, to fold their legs into the carapace (head and chest region) forming a protective ball shape. This may well give them some protection from birds, since the spiders can remain motion-less for minutes with a less leggy, and therefore less spidery appearance. Looked at under a magnifying lens, such a specimen presents rather a comic sight – eight bright little eyes peering out through a cage of legs.

The ability of the legs to grasp like human fingers allows the free-living hunting spiders to catch and hold on to their prey. They are aided in this task by having the extremities of the legs furnished below or at the tip with a thick brush of hairs called a *scopula*. The end of each individual hair is split into thousands of filaments that are covered in a thin film of moisture, enabling them to stick to smooth surfaces. The spider's scopulae are very efficient – even some of the largest spiders can walk or hang on a sheet of the smoothest glass. In some families the scopulae are modified to hold on to prey rather than surfaces, but in both cases this brush of hairs allows the spider to retain its prey better once it has been caught.

All spiders have two claws terminating each leg; a few species have a single claw at the end of each palp as well. Unlike hunting spiders, weavers never have scopulae – instead they have, between the others, an additional claw with which they grip the lines of their web. The spiders that get trapped in our baths and hand-basins are always weavers – hunting spiders can easily walk up the slippery sides and continue their wanderings.

Booklungs and heartbeats

Insects breathe through *trachea* – tiny tubes that penetrate into the body and are responsible for the diffusion of oxygen. In addition, spiders are equipped with lungs: mygalomorphs have two pairs, araneomorphs a single pair. They are formed of tiny leaves like the pages of a book and are known as *booklungs*. The breathing system is not very efficient in spiders, particularly in the larger species, which soon become breathless if forced to run very far. Spiders are masters of the fast attack, but whilst they are remarkable in being able to move swiftly after being totally motionless for long periods, they cannot, in general, sustain such activity for more than a few seconds.

The spider's heart is to be found at the front end of the abdomen and it is often marked by a longitudinal patch. This patch, where it exists,

forms part of the pattern on the spider's back. In an exhausted spider, the heart can be seen pulsating by means of the regular motions of the white parts of the pattern. Larger spiders have slower heart beats (50 per minute) than smaller ones (more than 100 per minute) and an active spider can increase its heart rate by a factor of nearly four times over the resting state.

Spiders and man

The large mygalomorphs that feature in film and television as the personification of the deadly animal are chosen mainly because their larger size makes them easier to film. If anything they are less poisonous than their smaller relatives, relying on their size and strength rather than poison. However, some of the mygalomorphs have, on their abdomens, special hairs they can brush off with their rear legs. If these get inhaled or penetrate the skin, they can have an unpleasant effect like the hairs of nettles. For this reason they are known as *urticating* hairs, from the scientific name of the nettle – *Urtica*.

Spiders are so conditioned to feeding on insects that they are most unlikely to bite us except in self-defence. Many spiders will nip if held in the

Above: the poison of Thomisus onustus *is fatal to insects but harmless to man. Here, its bright colouring provides camouflage on a flower*

fingers, but if allowed to walk over our hand they will do just this and are no more likely to bite us than they would attack the ground or vegetation on which they walk. Although the Black Widow spider has been implicated in numerous cases of envenomation in America, I once kept one and found it to be a timid creature. On several occasions it accompanied me to lectures where I demonstrated its ability to pull in its legs and feign death, which it did at the lightest touch. I have also had the European Black Widow walk harmlessly across my hand while I was trying to photograph it in its retreat. Yet in the same circumstances I have been bitten by a *Thomisus* crab spider who was guarding her eggs, and also by a *Chiracanthium* spider emerging from her egg sac. Now, *Thomisus* has a poison that acts swiftly on large bees, and whilst I felt the prick of its fangs, I could see no signs of the bite and felt no effects whatever. Some *Chiracanthium* species are reckoned to be poisonous to man but again I suffered no ill-effects. If only mosquito bites were so innocuous!

SPIDER VAGRANTS

'. . . they toil not neither do they spin'
St Matthew 6:28

Naturalists divide spiders into three broad ecological groups. The first of these, web-builders, live in or near their webs and rely on them to snare their prey passively. The other two, tube dwellers and vagrant hunters, depend on active assault to overwhelm their victims, but while tube dwellers do their hunting from the security of a permanent base, vagrants build only temporary retreats – and some have no permanent home at all.

In the popular imagination, spiders and webs are inseparable, but there are numerous species that make little use of silk to catch their prey – these are the vagrant hunters. Some are active only during the daytime and depend mainly on their keen sight, while others work only at night, groping about in the dark until something they can eat wanders near. Although it might seem extraordinary that a hunting animal should be virtually blind, most of the spiders that hunt at night appear to have lost the use of their eyes in favour of their finely-tuned tactile senses: vibrations caused by potential prey are relayed to them through the

The flies seeking a meal in this bloom are themselves about to become food for the wandering crab spider Diaea dorsata

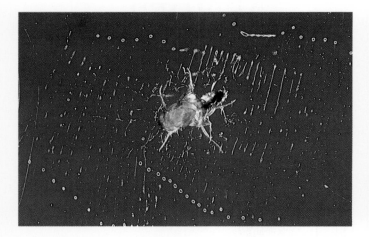

Above: S. thoracica *does not need an accurate aim to shoot its gluey poison, since the liquid spreads widely. The fly is consumed through a tiny puncture, and only a husk is left (top)*

Above: *well-camouflaged, the central American species* Sicarius rugosus *burrows into the sand to await its prey. Here, a doomed beetle larva has blundered into the buried hunter*

vegetation on which the spiders climb, or picked up through the air by the fine hairs (*trichobothria*) that occur near the extremities of their legs. Once their prey is located, many hunting spiders use highly specialised procedures for disabling and devouring it.

Sticky threads

Although its original habitat is under stones and in deep vegetation in southern Europe, one of the most interesting hunters, the Spitting Spider or *Scytodes thoracica* is now found in houses in the north of the continent as well, and it has even been transported to America and Australia, where it has also become a domestic spider. *Scytodes* has developed a predatory technique not found in any other genus of spider. When prey is sensed at a distance of a couple of centimetres, the spider turns to face it and gives a rapid shudder, firing strong, sticky threads composed of a mixture of poison and glue

that leave its victim rooted to the spot, struggling to escape. *Scytodes* then cautiously steps forward and administers a poisonous bite. The hunter needs the advantage of this immobilisation since its chelicerae are small and parallel, incapable of much lateral movement. The fangs are also quite tiny so the spider is able to bite only a leg or a wing.

These spiders use this special weapon for both attack and defence, and seem to catch most of what comes into range, but a serious drawback is that prey must first chance to approach very closely before the method can be called into use.

Deadly concealment

Because the number and arrangement of their eyes is similar to *Scytodes*, sicariid spiders were once grouped with them by arachnologists but these latter, known as 'six-eyed crab spiders', are quite different in appearance and technique from the Spitting Spider.

Imagine a sandy, tropical location; a luckless insect is making its way across the sand, intent on finding food. Suddenly it is surrounded from below by six knobbly legs, stabbed with poisonous fangs and held fast – *Sicarius rugosus* (the six-eyed crab spider has found its meal for the day. The colour and texture of this spider are very similar to those of the sandy soil; it buries itself just below the surface, forelegs exposed but well camouflaged. Perhaps it can feel the vibrations as its prey approaches, or possibly it reacts rapidly when its victim unwittingly touches it. Sight certainly plays no part, because the spider's eyes are covered with sand along with the rest of its body.

Above: Thomisus onustus *is known for its predation of bees. The spider strikes at the 'neck', avoiding the sting and sending its poison straight to the main nervous system*

Above: Xysticus kochi *sometimes preys on the weevils that threaten plants and stored produce* Overleaf: *a hoverfly falls victim to the crab spider* Misumena vatia *lurking on a seed head*

Also known as crab spiders, the *Thomisidae* family will eat almost any kind of prey, regardless of size. If we can spot this spider waiting for its meal (and this is not always easy since it is shaped and coloured to match the plants it lives among) we notice first that although its eyes are small and widely separated, the spider sees us and extends its heavy front legs. As we get closer, it possibly thinks this is the biggest insect it has ever seen! Closer still and any anticipation it might have had of a large meal turns into the suspicion that we might be a predator, and the spider scuttles off sideways, just like a diminutive crab. Crab spiders are the antithesis of the general image of a hunter, since they tend to be rather stout and slow-witted creatures. They are by no means blind, but their sight is not good and their chelicerae are tiny – so how do they manage to thrive? Their weapons are patience and a poison strong enough to paralyse formidable insects like bees, or strong flyers such

as butterflies. In addition, some of the 'crabs' (those known as flower spiders) conceal themselves in the blooms and ambush visiting insects. Not only do these species match the colour of the petals, but many have curious shapes that mimic plant forms and so help to disguise their presence.

Once a large insect is caught, the spider holds it with the first two pairs of legs, which are particularly long and strong. It then administers a bite at the junction of the insect's head and thorax. Once the quick-acting, virulent poison has paralysed the prey, the spider's legs release their hold and it is gripped solely with the fangs.

As with some other hunting spiders, the prey's corpse appears totally unmarked after the 'crab' has finished with it.

Varied diet

Xysticus is a genus of crab spider that has a large number of species scattered around the world.

Above: *the divergent chelicerae and long fangs of* Dysdera crocata *allow it to penetrate the tough dorsal plates of a woodlouse.*

Most of these feature various shades of brown markings, which serve them well since they forage on the ground and among low plants. Unlike their gaudier relatives, *Xysticus* spiders do not come into contact with particularly large, powerful adversaries, but they will eat an astonishing variety of prey, some of which is seldom if ever tackled by other hunting spiders: winged ants, weevils and other small beetles all feature on their menu. Well-armoured prey like these have only one weak spot in their design – the articulations of the legs, where the cuticle is thinner to allow for bending – and this is the precise point where *Xysticus* buries its fangs.

Another spider that has six eyes like *Sicarius* and *Scytodes* is, like the latter, cosmopolitan, and has its origins in the Mediterranean region. This is *Dysdera*, a garden spider, which is one of the few hunting species that catch and eat woodlice. These land crustaceans pull in their many legs and hold themselves down when threatened, and whereas most spiders would be quite incapable of piercing or even gripping their tough dorsal plates, *Dysdera*

has such long fangs that they can be pushed under the edge of these plates to lever the woodlouse up. Once the softer underside is accessible, the spider can pierce it with his fangs and inject it with poison. Fortunately for *Dysdera*, the smallness of its appetite and the density of the woodlouse population ensure that it never faces a food shortage.

The flesh-coloured abdomen and reddish carapace of *Dysdera* give it a distinctive and rather unpleasant appearance. It is one spider I would not be happy to handle, since its spreading chelicerae are capable of giving a nasty nip to a human as well as an insect.

Intrepid fighters
Many spiders, including such comparatively aggressive species like *Dysdera crocata*, will avoid encounters with ants, but more interestingly, there are a few spiders who actually live solely or mainly on these aggressive little creatures. Some species of ant-preying spider mimic their prey in behaviour or appearance, although the reasons for this remain a matter of scientific conjecture. One of these is *Callilepis*, a small genus of spider (found in Europe, America, India and Japan) that has

evolved a unique method of dealing with them. When *Callilepis* encounters a potential meal, it adopts a stance geared for a quick lunge, raising its front legs to locate the insect's antennae, and then making a quick bite at their base. The ant is fairly aggressive when it meets the much larger spider, but on being bitten it is even more fierce, so the spider immediately retreats to await the curious event that subsequently takes place. The poison acts first on the antennae, which soon become limp and useless so that in the death throes that follow, the ant turns helplessly in circles, no doubt because of the loss of sensitivity in these organs. Mortally wounded, it cannot run away, and eventually the spider returns, this time to deliver a longer bite. Once the ant is completely paralysed, *Callilepis* grips it in its fangs and carries it away from any other ants, to a spot it has previously covered over with silk for protection. The spider feeds through one or two small bites on the neck and abdomen of the ant, which is left as an empty husk after a couple of hours.

Zodarion, another exclusive ant predator, is found mainly in Europe and North Africa, and the most telling evidence of its presence is the piles of dead ants it leaves beneath stones. These spiders

Above: C. schuszteri *is unusual in eating ants, which often prey on spiders. Ants also contain formic acid, which repels most vagrants*

Above: *the glossy bodies and slender legs of* Zodarion *spiders give them a similar appearance to the ants on which they prey*

have a very similar method of attack to *Callilepis*, although their fatal bite is normally aimed at antennae rather than the body, since they have only small, feeble chelicerae that are joined at the base and so cannot open very far.

It is remarkable that such ill-equipped hunters are not only *capable* of tackling ants (among the most pugnacious of insects) – they actually *specialise* in them.

High jumpers

The *Salticidae* are the largest family of spiders and its members are popularly known as jumping spiders or 'jumpers'. Among arachnologists they are regarded with some affection as they have good eyesight and an engaging curiosity.

On one occasion I was trying to photograph a

male *Heliophanus* that seemed to have a pressing engagement elsewhere. Hoping to frighten him into a standstill so that I could get my shot, I blocked his path with my free hand. Undeterred, he jumped straight onto it, so I flipped my wrist to propel him back onto the ground. He landed facing away from me, and then turned towards me, his eyes looking me up and down in such a disdainful way that I was really sorry I had been so rough with him!

The salticid eyes can certainly spot a large object like a human at several feet, but smaller fry such as its normal prey must be closer before it is noticed. When the 'jumper' sees a possible meal nearby, it begins to stalk it in a kitten-like way, running a few steps and stopping, its palps working up and down as if in delight at the prospect of a meal. In

Below: *jumping spiders have a remarkably flexible prosoma that enables their eyes to be turned in different directions*

Above: *wolf spiders such as* Alopecosa fabrilis *can reach lengths of 25mm, and have strong enough chelicerae to tackle even very heavily armoured insects such as beetles*

vegetation, the spider will leap from twig to leaf to follow its prey, but on a smoother surface the stalking is done in a series of short dashes interspersed with sudden stops. All the time the prey is transfixed by the large eyes, and when it is within range, the spider leaps upon it. If, as frequently happens, the prey is aware of the spider's approach and flies off a split second before the leaping spider reaches it, the spider is left in a professionally embarrassing situation. It does not look around for the missing insect as we might in such circumstances, but carefully wipes its eyes with its palps before moving away.

Salticidae are unique among jumping animals in that they lack a greatly enlarged pair of back legs, yet many are prodigious leapers and one species *Attulus saltator* can span a distance greater than twenty times its own length when it is threatened. All spiders have muscles in their legs, but these can only bend the leg, not stretch it; the jumping spiders accomplish their leaps by means of a hydraulic mechanism that inflates the limbs and causes them to be stretched.

Skillful hunters

The wolf spiders (those of the family *Lycosidae*) are immediately recognisable from the arrangement of their eyes in three rows on the carapace – four small ones at the front, and two large ones in the middle and back rows respectively. The predatory behaviour of the lycosids is more varied than that of the saltacids: some are fairly similar in making a lunge towards their prey without any preliminary stalking, others hunt from burrows like mygalomorphs do, and yet others make sheet webs. Their eyesight is good, but not quite up to the standard of the jumping spiders, and, in complete contrast to that family, some of the larger species of wolf spider are nocturnal.

In northern Europe they are typified by the genus *Pardosa*, small active spiders that frequent the ground. One species, *Pardosa lugubris*, is particularly numerous in and around woods, and it is often possible to hear them scampering about on the dry, fallen leaves. They do not actively chase their prey, although they are good runners and can make small leaps to speed themselves along the ground. Unlike jumping spiders, which spring from a standing start, 'wolves' incorporate

their leaps into a run; even so, they never jump farther than a few body lengths.

The largest British wolf spider is *Alopecosa fabrilis*, widespread in Europe but occurring in England only on two sandy heaths in the south. The chelicerae of *Alopecosa* are large and powerful, and this spider probably depends more on its strength than on the potency of its poison. Certainly, it can cope easily with large flies and it has a strange method of doing so; once it catches the fly, the spider holds it down with its front legs much like a dog would, while stabbing it quickly with the chelicerae. The spider immediately turns a somersault, landing on its back with the struggling fly held aloft. Removing the fly's feet from the ground and grasping its wings, the spider thus ensures that it has no means of escape and, if necessary, *Alopecosa* can reposition its fangs or make slight adjustments to its grip without any fear of the fly getting away. In less than a second the spider rights itself, its victim held firmly by the chelicerae alone.

The burrow of *Alopecosa fabrilis* consists of a closed cell, thinly walled with silk, just below the surface of the sand. Species of the genus *Arctosa* dig a longer tube, sometimes T or Y-shaped, with a thin silk curtain across the entrance. Some lycosids, like the American genus *Geolycosa*, make burrows as deep as one metre; the Australian 'wolves' have shallower burrows but use their silk to attach small pieces of vegetation around the entrance. Other species build a simple mound at the opening to prevent flood-water from entering; yet others adopt the mygalomorph idea of a front door, thick or thin as the case may be (see Chapter 4). All these burrowing lycosids spend their days below ground and at night either sit at their thresholds waylaying passing insects, or wander nearby, grabbing anything they meet.

Fishing for prey

Also known (inaccurately) as wolf spiders are the *Pisauridae* family. None of these make burrows and all are substantial in size but they are not confined to the ground like true wolf spiders. The Swamp or Fisher Spiders of the genus *Dolomedes* are found near water, although immature individuals of the European species *Dolomedes fimbriatus* can be abundant in the foliage of nearby trees. The

Opposite: *found only in or near damp places,* Dolomedes *spiders will take large prey such as minnows which they attract by vibrating the water with their front legs*

habitat of *Dolomedes* has been severely reduced in England – unfortunately, for this is one of the most impressive of English spiders – the powerfully built body can be up to 22mm long in the female.

Dolomedes spiders use the water's surface like a web to transmit the vibrations of potential prey as they station themselves with their forelegs resting on it and their rear legs hanging on to poolside vegetation. Their usual victims are insects, but on occasion they will actually catch fish. The front legs tap the surface of the water, attracting the attention of an insectivorous fish below, and when it comes up to eat what it supposes to be a drowning fly, it is itself grasped by the spider and paralysed by its poison. These spiders will attack not only fish that are marginally bigger than themselves, but also tadpoles and small frogs. In spite of their audacity in tackling these small vertebrates however, they are timid where humans are concerned and will dive below the surface and stay there for several minutes to avoid us.

Tiny wanderers

Before we leave the hunting spiders we should look at some of the midget members of the *Linyphiidae* family – the Money Spiders, whose ballooning behaviour we examined in Chapter 1. Not all of these make webs; some live in leaf litter or tall vegetation and wander about looking for prey in the same manner as many of their larger relatives. As with most hunting spiders, their prey is never larger than themselves, and springtails (small wingless insects) make up a high proportion of their diet. It is also these abundant creatures that figure prominently on the menu for the earliest stages of the most of the other hunting spiders, all of which begin their careers as spiderlings of two or three millimetres in length. The Money Spiders never get any bigger than this and are no more than one millimetre long when they catch their first meal. There is little competition between them and other hunters though, for there is plenty of prey for all. These midgets, in any case, are mostly hatched in the spring when other species tend to be fully grown. This means that in any particular season the spiders in each stage of their development will be hunting for prey of a different size. Furthermore, Money Spiders stay in action throughout the colder months of the year, so that while most other spiders are tucked away for the winter, the linyphiids have unrestricted access to their own small prey – in the northern hemisphere a number are even active under snow.

TUBE
AND
TENT
DWELLERS

'Will you walk into my parlour?' said a
spider to a fly;
''Tis the prettiest little parlour that ever you
did spy.'

Mary Howitt, nineteenth century

Some tube dwellers spin a cylindrical home above ground, but most hollow their retreat out of the earth, and some of the most fascinating of these are the *Ctenizidae* or 'trap-door' spiders. Their behaviour, predatory characteristics and especially the protective devices they have developed to elude their enemies, are extremely varied and complex, but the existence of all ctenizid spiders revolves around the tube or burrow which, as is the case with all tube dwellers, provides not only protection, but a place of hiding from which it can strike out at its prey.

The construction of this burrow, with its silk lining and hinged door, is therefore a vital and complicated feat of engineering, and one for which the spider is ably fitted. The ctenizids have a smooth and rather glossy appearance, but closer observation of the chelicerae reveals a rake of thick, short, spiny setae that are used, with the fangs, to scratch a tunnel out of the earth. The industrious builder compresses the dug-out soil into a pellet, carries it to the entrance, then pushes

Ctenizidae *like this eastern Mediterranean species have a slow growth rate since they feed only on prey that comes within reach of their burrows*

Above and top: *because it is weathered and colonised by vegetation exactly like the surrounding soil, the earth door of a* Cteniza *burrow is very difficult to discover*

open the 'door' to fling it out. These remarkable doors are of two types, known respectively as 'cork' and 'wafer'. The cork door is thick and has a bevelled edge that fits the rim of the burrow exactly, whereas the wafer door is thinner, without a bevel, but it is manufactured with the same precision. Both types are composed of soil particles cemented together with saliva and bound up with silk; the spider begins to mould the door at its hinge and gradually extends it until it is the same size as the opening of the tube. The spider then feels around the perimeter of the door to detect any irregularities, and fills these with additional pieces of soil. When this has been completed, the spider pulls the door tightly shut, helping to give it a perfect fit. The door is added to periodically whenever the burrow is enlarged, so that older, more established spiders have larger and thicker doors to their burrows than their juniors, or those in newer dwellings. All of the cork doors are heavy

enough to slam shut with their own weight after the spider disappears back into its burrow after one of its rare excursions, so that even specimens living in captivity are rarely seen. In addition, the burrows are extremely difficult to find when the doors are closed as these match their surroundings in soil type and even have the same sort of moss or other small plants growing on top. If you are interested in the well-being of a particular specimen, one way of ensuring that it is still alive is to prop open the door of its burrow with a small twig: if it is still ajar the following morning, fear the worst! If the spider is alive and well it will have removed the obstruction during the night and regained its privacy.

Defensive tactics

Although these spiders are known as *trap-door* spiders, the door is not part of a trap, since a real trap-door would collapse under the weight of an insect and let it fall to the waiting fangs of the spider beneath. *These* doors on the other hand, open outwards, and are designed, as we have seen, to protect the occupant of the burrow from the outside world. They are the first line of defence against the spider's smaller adversaries, such as scorpions, centipedes, pompilid wasps and some flies, as well as larger ones like birds and mammals. In some species, the lower parts of the third pair of legs are modified into shallow U-shapes and furnished with many small spines at their extremities. When a predator approaches, these legs are held above the spider's body and pressed tightly against the walls of its tubular burrow, while the fangs hold on to the underside of the door, preventing the entry of all but the strongest enemy. Even when a knife blade is inserted, the pressure required to raise the door is considerable; one experiment showed that a spider was able to resist an upward force of 38 times its own weight!

If this fails, a trap-door spider with a simple tube burrow is at the mercy of the intruder, but some species, such as the Australian *Anidiops villosus* have another trick up their sleeves. The burrow is lined, as are most, with a layer of silk adhering to the walls. About half way down the tube is a spot that the spider habitually uses as a midden, breaking the silk at that point and placing the remains of its meals 'under the carpet'; having put its rubbish out of sight, it then re-weaves the silk. Should an enemy penetrate the door, the spider rushes down the burrow and pulls down the silken sleeve it has built up around the midden. This

Above: Anidiops villosus *stores its 'leftovers' behind a break in the silken lining of its burrow. When invaded, the spider pulls the loose sleeve down and releases the debris*

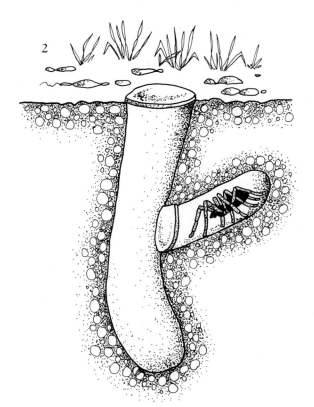

Above: *trap-door spiders from many different families protect themselves from predators and flash floods by building an extra chamber with a second door into the side of the main burrow*

makes a seal across the bottom section of the tube, under which the spider skulks, while the rubbish from out of the walls falls on top (figure 1). When the predator reaches what he believes to be the bottom of the tube and finds only dessicated leftovers, it wanders off to search elsewhere.

One compatriot of *Anidiops, Stanwellia nebulosa*, operates a superior form of this disappearing act in which a pellet of compacted earth is stored in the side pocket, making an even more substantial barrier.

Another escape technique is employed by several American and Australian species, which make a side tunnel that itself is furnished with a door. If threatened, the spider rushes below the hanging, inner door and pushes it upward to seal off the upper part of the burrow. If the visitor is not fooled and persists in attempting to open this second door, the spider insinuates itself into the side tunnel while still holding the door up, then suddenly releases it and pulls it against its new hiding place (figure 2). The intruder's feelings of victory soon change to bewilderment and defeat when it finds the lower chamber as empty as the upper. More sophisticated still are the defences of a Venezuelan spider, *Rhytidicolus structor*, which uses no less than three doors to escape its enemies. The outer door leads to an enlarged urn-shaped chamber where the spider waits to pounce or defend, while below this a second door leads to an elongated chamber, which in turn has an inner sanctum half way along, with a third door in it (figure 3).

In spite of the capacity some members of the trap-door family have for complex construction work, others seem to have given up hope of living to tell the tale if they remain in their burrow when invaded by a predatory scorpion or wasp. Their tubes have a simple side tunnel leading up to ground level, camouflaged by a pile of loose earth. If the spider is threatened by a frontal attack it scrambles through the back door and makes its escape through the undergrowth. Even simpler in design is the burrow of another South American spider, *Stothis astuta*, obviously a nervous creature that hedges its bets by making a U-shaped burrow with identical doors at both ends, so that unless it is attacked simultaneously by two predators, it can make a fast exit by either door (figure 4).

One genus of these less ambitious engineers that has developed a particularly astounding method of protective camouflage is *Cyclocosmia*, found in shady ravines in the south-eastern states of the

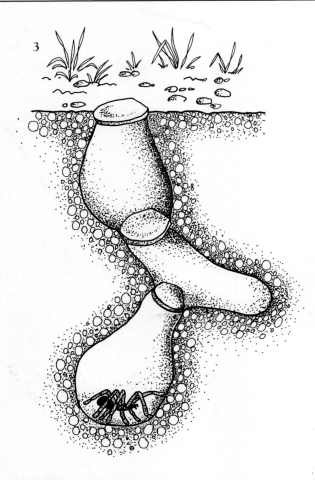

Above: Rhytidicolus structor *from Venezuela provides an even better defence by constructing two further side chambers in its lair. Wily predators that have solved the two-door trick may be fooled by the third door!*

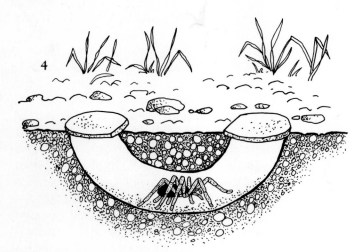

Above: *the U-shaped burrow of the thick-set Caribbean species* Stothis astuta *is almost certainly made this way for defence rather than aggression, but does its construction give two chances to invaders or the fleeing spider?*

USA, in eastern Mexico and in Indochina. Its appearance is particularly distinctive since it has a flattened rear end with a leathery texture and grooves radiating from the centre. The spider makes a plain vertical burrow with a thin, hinged door and a shape that tapers gently downward; when it is invaded, the occupant dives to the bottom, where its broadened posterior fits the diameter of the tube exactly. A predator dashes in to search for the spider, but finds the burrow apparently empty, not realising that the base of the tube is the back end of the spider (figure 5).

From the diversity of their defences, it is obvious that even these spiders, among the largest known, have their share of trials and tribulations. As well as guarding against predators, the 'doors' are a first defence against flash floods and effectively seal the burrow against climatic fluctuations, maintaining a more even temperature and humidity than would be possible out in the open.

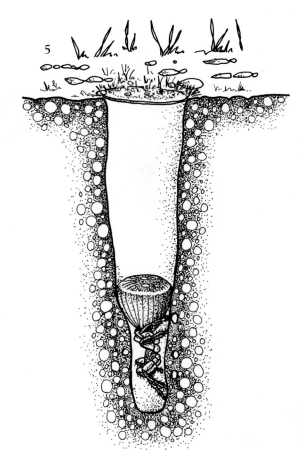

Above: Cyclocosmia's *amazing ability to disguise its rear end as the floor of its burrow protects it from most predators. Some parasitic wasps however can not only see through the ruse, but also penetrate the spider's leathery hide*

Above: *the cribellate silk lining of* Filistata insidiatrix's *burrow is combed out into curly strands that will snare any unwary insect*

Above: F. insidiatrix *seems to be sluggish in attacking its prey; it searches for a leg or wing to bite before dragging the insect to its lair*

Hidden dangers

The trap door spider passes its day in the depth of its hole; at night it lurks near the door, ready to catch its prey with a sudden darting movement from underneath it. A few species will wander a very short distance at night, but most will emerge no further than they can reach while clinging with their legs over the entrance so the door is worn like a flat cap shading their gleaming eyes; others are completely hidden, just below the door.

A variation on the hunting technique of the trap-door spiders is practised by *Filistata*, a cribellate genus found in warm climates that, unlike most tube dwellers, is an araneomorph rather than a more primitive mygalomorph. This spider spins distinctive coiled threads that radiate from the burrow and immediately snare any insect foolish enough to come into contact with it.

The ecribellate genus *Segestria*, and the very similar *Ariadna*, also spin strands that radiate from their nesting places, but these serve a different purpose; their long lines of plain silk signal the presence of moving prey to the spider which waits out of sight, deep within its horizotal tube. Unlike other tube-dwellers, and indeed other spiders, *Segestria* and *Ariadna* have three pairs of legs directed forward, only the rear pair pointing backwards. If this arrangement is designed to help

Above: Segestria florentina *preys on flies that sun themselves on the walls near which the spider builds its web. Long radiating lines signal the presence of the moving insect*

them move more quickly out of the tube and along the silken lines, then it is very effective, for they are the fastest of all weaving spiders. The only sure way to discover the precise identity of the owner of one of these distinctive webs is to tickle one of the radiating strands and hope that the occupant of the burrow is fooled into showing itself. Sometimes the spider can be seen cautiously approaching the mouth of the tube but often it comes out as if jet-propelled, probes the vibrating strand, reverses direction without turning and then disappears – all in a fraction of a second. On one occasion, I crouched down to observe the large European *Segestria florentina* near the bottom of a wall. After I had spent a minute or so tickling the web, the spider suddenly advanced with such speed that I

was literally bowled over. By the time I had picked myself up it was deep within its tube again, and further fruitless tickling showed that it had got wise to me. These spiders often look remarkably large for the size of the burrow they occupy, but they have no need for space to turn around in as they can run backwards just as fast as forwards.

Family patterns

When they survive the perils of the natural world, trap-door spiders in particular are very long-lived, and a fortunate female might spend twenty years or more living in her hole in the ground. The males mature after several years of this existence, then suddenly vacate their prisons for a brief airing above ground when they search for a female – in good seasons they can be seen in huge numbers. Mating takes place in the female's burrow and in due course she lays eggs; the newly hatched spiderlings spend several months with their mother before wandering a short distance and digging

Above: *the Mediterranean tent builder* Uroctea durandi *is beetle-like in shape and markings. If forcibly ejected from its home, it scuttles to the nearest crevice much like a beetle would*

Inset: *the spider's retreat is commonly found suspended a few millimetres below a large rock. The signal lines are also suspended on silk pylons so vibrations are relayed straight to the spider*

their own burrows. Two Australian species are known to balloon and can travel over considerable distances, but the majority disperse on foot, thus forming closely grouped colonies.

A safe retreat

Related to the tube dwellers are the spiders known as 'tent dwellers'. Their retreats (the design of which would appear to be a modification of those tubular homes that are spun above ground) are convex silken structures with several openings. These 'tents', which should not be confused with the tent-like retreats suspended in the webs of certain sheet web builders such as *Cyrtophora* (see Chapter 5), are often found in corners in houses or under rocks and stones.

A typical tent-dwelling species is *Uroctea durandi*, a Mediterranean spider that lives in rocky places. The retreat of *Uroctea* incorporates a feature that occurs elsewhere among other tent builders as well as some tube dwellers, as we have seen – signal or tripping lines radiating from the main entrance to the retreat that serve to alert the occupant to the presence of its prey.

Interestingly, *Uroctea* and some other tent-builders like the much smaller *Oecobius*, throw strong bands of silk around the prey, completely wrapping it before carrying it back to the retreat to be eaten. This behaviour, and the radiating strands of the web, give weight to the idea that the orb weavers described in Chapter 6 have evolved from spiders like these.

SHEET AND TANGLE

'. . . the newest houses, the first day they are whited, will have both Spiders and Cobwebs in them'.

Rev. E. Topsell, 1607 (after T. Mouffet)

Although the term 'spider's web' normally brings to mind the familiar circular 'orb' construction, there are many species that build webs of different types. Some of these have a random tangled appearance, while others take the form of a smooth sheet of silken strands, and a few species make webs that combine both of these designs. Certain spiders live permanently on their sheets, but many spend the day in tubular retreats attached to their webs; one of the best-known of these is *Tegenaria*, the European House Spider, whose 'home' we find in dark corners of rooms.

Because house spiders are so large and so recognisable, numerous stories have been told about encounters with them. On a number of occasions I have heard of 'pets' (with names like Sidney or Sam) emerging from below the family sofa every evening, apparently to watch television. In fact, their transparent sheet web will have been made on the carpet and the near-blind spider comes to wait for prey, oblivious of the giants around him – and the entertainment!

Summoned by their mother with a tug on her tangled web, immature Theridion sisyphium *spiders feed on a hoverfly she has killed*

Above: *modern, centrally-heated homes are too dry to be ideally suited to* Tegenaria gigantea. *Here a thirsty specimen takes a drink*

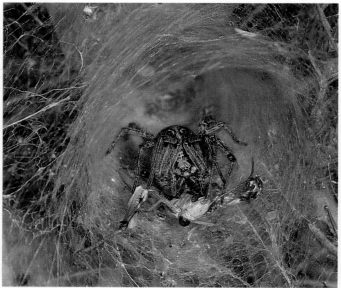

Above: *the extensive sheet web and superstructure built by* Agelena labyrinthica *in low bushes is a perfect trap for grasshoppers*

Struggle to the end

A genus closely related to the House Spiders, *Agelena*, gives its name to the family that contains them both – the *Agelenidae*. The web of *A. labyrinthica* has a much larger sheet than that of its domestic cousins, and this is held in place by an extensive superstructure of tangled lines above it. This also functions as a trap for low-flying or leaping insects, which are caught in mid-flight and drop on to the sheet.

Imagine a grasshopper, for example, falling on the sheet, its legs poking through the fine holes. It attempts to leap to safety but because of its uncertain foothold cannot jump with much force; it hits the tangled skein above the web and lands back on the sheet. Once the grasshopper is exhausted by its struggles, the spider runs effortlessly across the web and gives the unfortunate creature a nip on one of its legs. It backs off and then repeatedly attacks from different angles, rather like a dog would. Once the poison has begun to take effect and the grasshopper's movements have subsided, the spider grips it in its fangs, pulls it back to the mouth of its tube and begins to enjoy its meal.

Agelenids have a world-wide distribution, represented in North America by *Agelenopsis* and several other species in closely related genera. The majority of this family are found in the northern hemisphere, but Australia has *Corasoides*, which makes similar webs to *Agelena*, and occurs in the same habitats – low bushes and grassy plots. In New Zealand the allied genus *Cambridgea* was once classed with the agelenids but is now grouped with the *Stiphidiidae*. A common species on the South Island, *C. antipodiana*, is a large long-legged spider that wanders into houses, its size and habits no doubt explaining why it was formerly classified with the European House Spiders. This species also makes a sheet web, with a system of guy ropes above and below it that is reminiscent of the handywork of the very much smaller linyphiids (or money spiders), which are found mainly in the temperate parts of the northern hemisphere. By no means all of them make webs but the most conspicuous are those that make guyed sheets (like *Agelena*) but without the tubular retreat. Like *Cambridgea*, the linyphiids hang underneath the web and wait for prey to bump into the upper guy lines and fall on to the sheet. Then they run along below the web and bite their victims' legs as these protrude through the sheet, quickly paralysing the prey and dragging it through the silken membrane. *Linyphia triangularis* is the most numerous species of the family and probably the most common British spider. It is remarkably catholic in its choice of web sites, these ranging from ground level to several metres up and occurring in all types of habitat from open wind-swept heaths to the dark interiors of forests. From their very numbers it is safe to assume that they take a severe toll of insects in the summer and autumn.

Left: *an intruding spider like this immature hunter* Pisaura mirabilis *is just as helpless on the convex sheet web of* Linyphia triangularis *as any insect – and as quickly caught*

Below: *like many linyphiids,* L. montana *makes a sheet web with strands above it to strengthen the structure and entangle insects. When the prey drops on to the sheet, the spider attacks it from below, pulling it into the sheet as it is bitten and paralysed, then devoured*

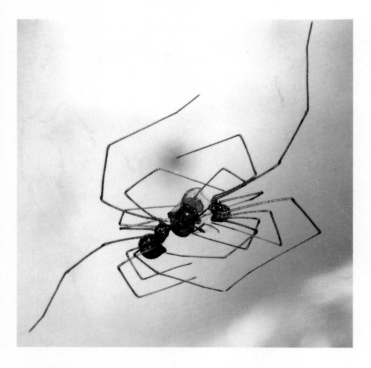

Above: *the typically long legs of these* Pholcus *spiderlings appear in danger of becoming permanently entangled as they share their prey*

Several members of the family make an extra sheet below the main one, the purpose of which seems to be the protection of the spider as it hangs in wait. Even some of the tiniest species, whose webs may be in a curled leaf lying on a woodland floor, put such a barrier web between themselves and the bottom of the leaf.

A silken trap
The pholcids are a family of spiders that have no separate sheet webs, but only a tangle of lines (some of them do, however, develop a small sheet or dome of silk within the tangle). *Pholcus phalangioides*, long in leg as well as name, is a house-dwelling species of the northern hemisphere, although found as well in rock crannies and caves in the warmer parts of its range. *Pholcus* has a fragile appearance, with a cylindrical abdomen and enormously long legs, and its web consists of widely-spaced strands, scattered apparently at random. The spider skulks at the top of the structure, in the darkest corner of the web, and in the evening it descends to the middle of its tangle and waits, in the typical inverted posture of the aerial weavers. If the web is touched and the spider knows that the vibrations in the strands are not caused by prey, it starts to gyrate its body at great speed as it retreats to the innermost part of its silky labyrinth; this alarming-looking behaviour is presumably an attempt to dislodge or frighten off the intruder.

These spiders have a wide range of prey, including moths, woodlice, and other spiders and when the prey gets entangled, *Pholcus* comes bounding along to it and then turns its back. Just as you are wondering whether this is a sign of rejection, you see the long legs throwing fine strands around the prey. This continues until the latter is well and truly enswathed, then the package is held with the claws on the spider's back legs and dragged off into the depths of the web, where it is devoured. *Pholcus* has small chelicerae, capable of very little movement, and the spider has to probe its parcel to find a thin extremity it can stab.

Lines of death
The *Theridiidae* are a world-wide family with many species, whose webs, like that of *Pholcus*, are three-dimensional tangles. *Theridion*, from which the family takes its name, has more species than any other genus, each of them small, with a glossy appearance and attractive colours and patterns. Some of these are found frequenting houses but most sling their webs on low plants and bushes. Unlike *Pholcus*, most of them make a small cup-shaped retreat where they live in the daytime, although like most spiders they come out on to the web at dusk. They will feed by night or day, snaring their prey on strands coated with a sticky secretion that holds the victim until the spider arrives. Like *Pholcus* and other aerial-web makers they turn their backs on their prey to wrap it securely in silk before taking it back to the retreat for consumption.

In America and Australia another theridiid – *Steatoda* – has become a common house-dweller. This is a distinctive genus of brownish spiders with a white band across the abdomen. Larger than most other theridiids and longer-lived than the majority of web-builders, they make a flat, horizontal sheet in the middle of their tangle webs. Those species living near ground level place taut silk lines running down from the sheet; these lines have globules of adhesive near the bottom and a weak link where the lines actually touch the ground. When an ant or beetle gets accidentally stuck on one of these sticky feet it starts to struggle and pull itself free. Suddenly the line breaks at the weakest point and hoists the insect up into the air where its wriggling brings it into contact with more of the glue. The spiders often have tubular retreats

Left: Theridion sisyphium, *a common spider in Europe, is one of several retreat builders that indulge in the particularly gruesome practice of fixing the cadavers of their victims to the outside of their shelters*

Below left: *a beetle* (Lagria hirta) *is killed and wrapped before being eaten by Steatoda bipunctata even though this insect, in common with many others, tries to deter potential predators by exuding a foul liquid from its joints*

Bottom left: *the tough silk retreat of the southern European 'Black Widow',* Latrodectus tredecimguttatus *reveals what a formidable spider it is. Attached to it are the empty husks of several beetles, all over 30mm in length; the spider is only half as long*

(like the agelenids) and come dashing out to haul in their catch, which, in common with all theridiids, they wrap in sticky silk – moderate amounts for smaller prey or large drops thrown on potentially dangerous insects.

Killers in black

The Black Widow spider *Latrodectus mactans* from the USA is also a theridiid and is one of the best known of the sheet-web builders. On numerous occasions it has inflicted painful bites, sometimes resulting in the death of its human victim, although the incidence of fatalities may formerly have been increased by the use of inappropriate antidotes.

The Widows are the largest of the theridiids at a maximum body length of 16mm, but a much smaller spider with a similar appearance – *Dipoena* – terrorizes even the most aggressive insects to be found in northern Europe. *D. tristis* is only a quarter of the length of *Latrodectus* and much smaller than its own prey, the Wood Ant *Formica rufa*; if this ferocious creature tumbles into the web of the diminutive *Dipoena* it is as good as dead. Sticky silk is thrown by the spider, which stays well clear of the ant's formidable jaws, and then a small bite is made in one of *Formica's* legs and the poison quickly takes effect. The ant's violent struggles soon cease and the spider seizes a leg and proceeds to reduce its victim to an empty husk. Most surprisingly, the spider can tolerate the ant's formic acid, the fumes from which can even kill the ant itself if it is kept in a confined space for a short while.

Above: *tiny but fierce,* Dipoena tristis *uses its potent venom to paralyse the much larger and equally aggressive European wood ant* Formica rufa *that has fallen into its web*

Diving bell

One of the most curious of the tangle-web weavers is *Argyroneta* – the water spider. It is unique in its habitat, being the only spider to live permanently under water, through which it swims gracefully, clothed in a silvery bubble of air that allows it to breathe in the same way as other spiders. The lines of its 'web' are attached to aquatic plants and keep its submarine retreat securely in place: this retreat is an inverted silken cup filled with air brought from the surface by the spider. In common with terrestrial species the water spider can only feed in air so the little aquatic creatures on which it feeds must be taken back to the bell before the meal can start. During the winter months it spends its time sealed in this bell, which is given extra layers of silk to prevent the air from escaping.

Fatal vision

A family of spiders that makes a strange and specialized use of its tangle web is *Dinopidae*. They have been given several common names – Ogre-faced, Retiarus or Net-casting spiders. The first rather unkindly refers to their enormous eyes and the last two names show that they make the most extraordinary web, and they use it in a way that could be out of science fiction.

The lanky spider flattens its body against a twig during the day and is perfectly camouflaged, but when night comes it begins to make a tangle of elastic threads below its perch. It orientates itself head upwards and, within a square framework of silk the size of a postage stamp, cards a series of cribellate strands across this frame. The spider then reverses its position and grips the four corners of the tiny sheet with its front legs, stretching it a few times as if testing its strength. When this is done, the spider waits. Although it is dark, the huge eyes can detect the slightest movement and when a beetle scurries below, the spider lunges down toward it, still holding the net, then scoops up the unfortunate creature in the sticky trap. A few more jerks by the spider and the beetle is completely entangled, wrapped for good measure, and eaten. This net-casting spider is unique in that while it is feeding it can begin to construct a new trap – the food is handled only by the palps.

Left: *the infamous 'Black Widow' of the USA,* Latrodectus mactans, *one of the few spiders that is dangerous to man. Early reports of spider-related deaths however, may have been increased by the many inappropriate cures administered*

Top: *fringes of hair below the legs (which may act as paddles) are all that distinguish* Argyroneta aquatica *from many land-based spiders*

Above: *with the onset of cold weather, A. aquatica adds extra layers of silk to its bell, making it perfectly air tight*

Left: Dinopis stauntoni *hangs face down with the net held between its legs, ready to drop it over any small insect passing below*

THE ORB WEAVERS

*'The spider as an artist has never been employed,
Though his surpassing merit is freely certified.'*

Emily Dickinson (c. 1873)

To the casual observer, the orb-web weavers might seem to represent almost the whole order of spiders, and because of their abundance and high visibility, more is known about their biology and ecology than any other comparable group. The typical orb web must be renewed daily, so there are plenty of opportunities to watch the complex process taking place, though it all happens so quickly that it is easy for the observer to overlook the finer points. Although closely related orb-weaving species make webs that are similar, the snares of many others are highly individual and an absent owner can often be identified solely by his handiwork. The webs can be found in almost every kind of habitat but the vast majority are stretched on bushes or strung between them.

Silken strength
It was the sight of a garden spider, *Araneus diadematus*, that first stimulated my own interest in spiders. The web of this species is very large compared with the size of the spider itself: an

Orb webs are complex and beautiful feats of engineering. The builder of this one is a European garden spider – Araneus diadematus

individual 18mm in body length can make a web 500mm in diameter, using up to 20 metres of silk line. Because of the fineness of the silk, the web is extremely light and the spider itself can be a thousand times as heavy as its own web. Not only does this structure support the spider – at rest and in motion – it is also capable of trapping strong, fast-flying insects.

Some of the largest and heaviest spiders (apart from the mygalomorphs) are found among the orb-web weavers. The heaviest European spider, for example, is another species of *Araneus* – *A. quadratus*. This is a large rotund species, normally reaching up to 15mm in body length, but in 1979 there was found on a heath in southern England a female 20mm long, weighing 2.25g. This giantess weighed four thousand times as much as her web!

A number of spiders in the genera *Cyclosa*, *Argiope* and *Uloborus* add dense ribbons of silk (known as *stabilmenta*) to their webs, and these appear to have a variety of functions. In some species they may be used to strengthen and stabilize the web (hence their name) but in the case of *Cyclosa* and *Uloborus* (spiders that live permanently on the hubs of their webs) they evidently serve as camouflage, since they blend perfectly

with the spiders' own patterning. These bands may also be used as moulting platforms or as shade from the sun and the cosmopolitan genus *Argiope* produces very showy stabilmenta designed to frighten off the birds or at least to deter them from flying through the webs. Most *Argiope* species are striped in yellow, white and black, a pattern that is common among arthropods and means 'Don't eat me – I taste unpleasant', and the banded stabilmenta of these spiders reinforce the message. Some orb-web weavers spend their whole lives sitting out on the hubs of their webs and making frequent forays to gather insects that blunder into them. Others silk together leaves to form a retreat, which is linked to the hub by silken lines that convey the vibrations of a struggling insect back to the spider. These retreats are normally hidden in

Top: *orb weavers know their craft from birth. Here, a young* Araneus diadematus *has built a web even more symmetrical than an adult's*

Right: *in a web it has adorned with warning flags of silk, the brightly-striped* Argiope bruennichi *spider sends a clear message to all potential predators – keep off!*

Above: *another spider that makes a stabilmentum is* Uloborus walckenaerius, *a cribellate species whose durable horizontal webs are not viscid*

Above: Cyclosa conica *from northern Europe builds a conspicuous vertical stabilmentum across the hub of its web*

nearby vegetation but a few species, such as *Metepeira labyrinthica*, build them in the webs themselves. (*Metepeira* also adds the protection of a tangle-web barrier to its web-based retreat).

A perilous flight

As might be expected, the great number of species of orb-web weavers has led to an extensive variety of web forms and modifications to the basic orb shape. Yet two spiders from opposite sides of the globe have evolved fascinatingly similar adaptations to deal with the same problem – catching the moths on which it lives.

Most moths are nocturnal and have developed various strategies to avoid night-active predators. As far as the sticky webs of the orb weavers are concerned, moths rely on the scales that cover their wings. When the moth touches a web the scales adhere, but they are easily shed, rendering the insect virtually 'non-stick'. A New Guinea spider, *Tylorida*, makes its orb web in the conventional way but in an extremely elongated shape, with the hub near the top. The upper radii are very short and the lower ones, forming in effect a ladder (the 'rungs' being the nearly horizontal sections of the spiral) are greatly lengthened (fig. 000). When a moth hits the web it falls down the ladder, progressively losing scales as it goes, until at last it is 'bald' and sticks to the web, where the spider can attack it. A Colombian Ladder Spider uses a very similar technique but in this case the hub is near the bottom of the web and the ladder stretches upwards from it.

Another New Guinea species, *Pasilobus*, uses a variant of the ladder principle to overcome the defences of the moths on which it feeds. The web has only three radii, which are strung out horizontally, and the 'hub' is merely the convergence point of the radii; the two dry lines that cross the web near this point form the spider's retreat. The viscid catching spiral in this case has been reduced to a dozen or so bridging threads sagging below the radii and loaded with gluey blobs. The spider waits in its retreat for the first moth of the night to fly into one of the sticky loops and become hopelessly entangled. It then dashes to the attack, biting and wrapping its prey before carrying it back to the retreat to be eaten.

Two more orb weavers specialize in moths – *Mastophora* in the Americas and *Dicrostichus* from Australia – but these two spiders have reduced their webs to a single line and each preys exclusively on one or two local species of moth, and

Above: *two spiders from opposite ends of the globe have evolved strangely similar methods for catching moths. By shedding wing-scales, moths often evade capture, but one species from New Guinea and another from Colombia get round this by building ladder-like extensions to their webs. In each case the moth tumbles down the 'rungs' and runs out of scales, but while the former ladder is below the hub of its web, the latter one is above it. The end result is the same however for the doomed moth*

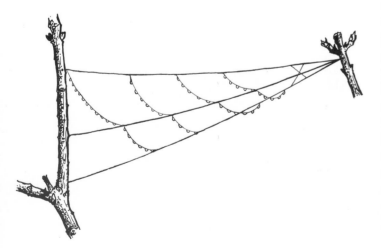

Above: Pasilobus, *also from New Guinea, has further refined the orb web. Making only three radii, the spider adds sticky cross-lines, each with a weak 'link'. When a moth hits a line the thread breaks at one end, the prey is left hanging and is soon caught by the spider*

then only the male insects. The spider makes a short thread covered with sticky material and then combs this glue down until a large blob is formed at the end of the thread – the bolas is ready. Experiments have shown that these spiders are able to mimic the sex pheromones (signal scent) of female moths and as the male insect approaches from down wind the spider detects the fluttering of his wings and starts swinging the sticky bolas – the hapless moth flies to its destruction. *Celaenia*, the Australian Orchard Spider, uses the same lure but merely dangles on a thread and grabs the moths as they fly in.

Ingenious constructions
One of the most eccentric of orb weavers is the rare *Paraplectanoides crassipes*, found in Tasmania and New South Wales. The 'barrier' web of this species consists of a thick wall in a shape reminiscent of a deflated football, which completely surrounds the orb web. The orb itself is much simplified, consisting solely of a thickened hub, connected to the outer wall by radiating lines, and a small hole is left in the barrier to arouse the curiosity of the springtails and cockroaches upon which the spider feeds. Once the insect is inside the ball, its movements are communicated by the radii to the waiting spider, which rushes along the nearest line to capture the prey and carry it back to the hub to be eaten.

Spiders of the genus *Hyptiotes* also make a web unlike any other. This is a mere slice of the normal web, not unlike that of *Pasilobus*, but strung vertically and made of dry silk. Four radii are joined by cribellate links, and the point of convergence of the radii is extended backwards in a single thread to the spider, which grips it with its front legs. The spider's rear legs hang on to a short strand of silk that anchors it to the branch of the tree in which it builds its web, and thus the spider itself makes a bridge. When prey hits the web, the spider's spinners let out silk, and the spider shoots forward so that the catching web partly collapses, entangling the prey in more lines. This continues until the spider reaches its victim and wraps it for later consumption.

Overleaf: *the body of* Hyptiotes paradoxus *forms a bridge between its anchor line and the single thread running to its web – a much-reduced orb not unlike that of* Pasilobus, *but strung in a more vertical plane than that of the New Guinea species and with four radii rather than three*

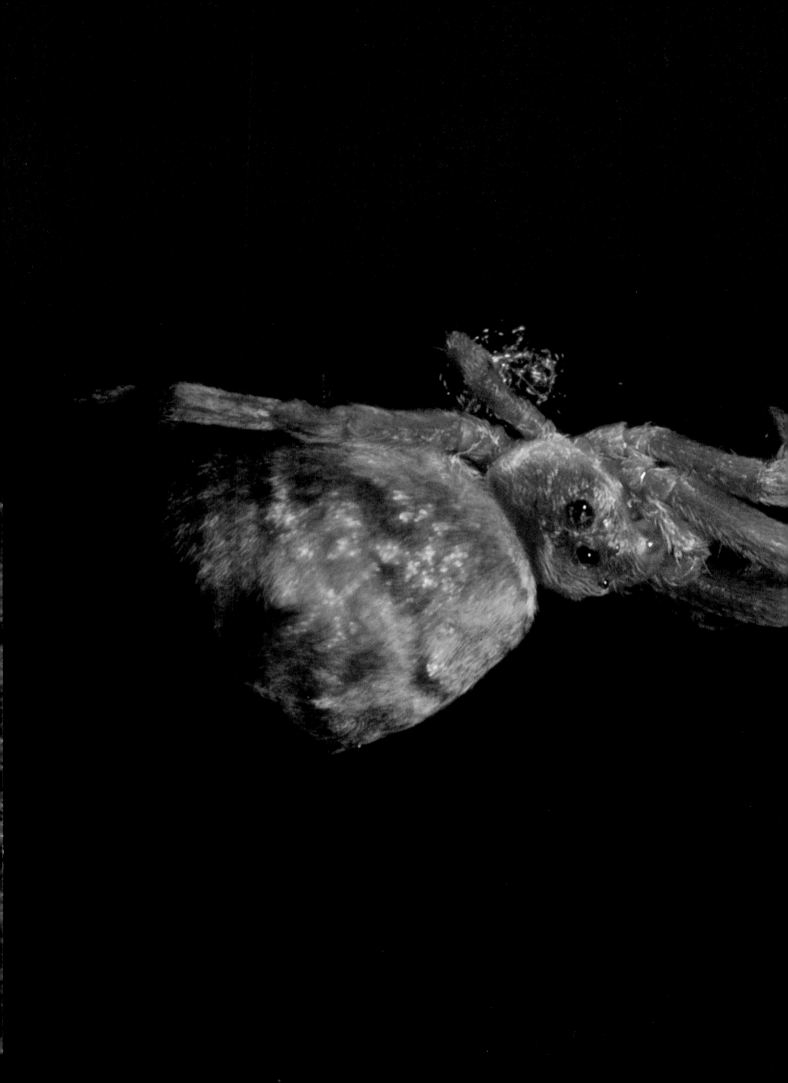

The orb web

The construction of this type of web, with its geometrical design, is a marvel of animal engineering that is accomplished within the space of half an hour. All of the steps in the process are instinctive and more or less unvarying; no use is made of vision, the spider employing only its delicate sense of touch to gauge the position and tension of the threads. The building of a web is often done at night, but if stormy weather prevents this the spider will build at the earliest opportunity, day or night.

The bridge

The spider's first move is to secure a bridge line, from which the finished web will hang, by spinning a long strand of silk and allowing it to stream out in the air. When the thread gets snagged on some piece of vegetation, which may be some way off or even on the other side of running water, the spider pulls on the line to see if it will bear its weight and then reinforces it by laying further strands of silk along it.

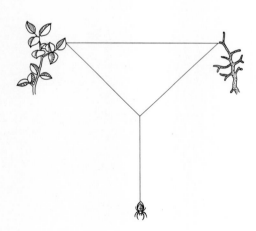

The Y-frame

Having made a suitably strong bridge line, the spider then runs along it, trailing a loose second line, which it fixes securely at each end of the bridge. Then it returns along this loose strand and spins a third thread vertically from its centre point. Pulling this third line down by its own weight the spider descends until it encounters a solid object,

to which it fixes the line. The spider has now established a basic framework in the shape of the letter Y – the centre of the Y will be the centre of the web.

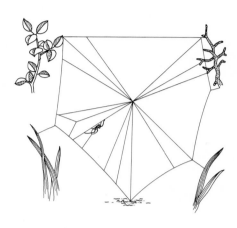

Frame lines and radii

The spider now returns to each end of the bridge and spins further frame lines, in which the web will ultimately be enclosed. By climbing along existing lines and trailing further lines behind, the spider then constructs more radii. Within a few minutes as many as 40 of these may be made, all carefully positioned to keep the tension in the web evenly balanced. Before the spider considers this phase to be complete it goes to the centre of the web and touches each radius in turn; any that are unsatisfactory are removed and repositioned. Tiny irregularities, quite undetectable to the human eye, are corrected at this stage.

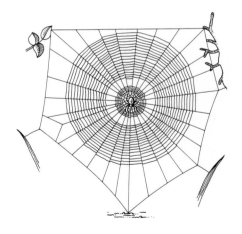

The hub

The spider now rotates at the centre of the web, spinning a tight spiral of silk. This is the hub, a central platform that is complete when its diameter is somewhat larger than the spider's leg-span.

The temporary spiral

Leaving an open zone around the edge of the hub, the spider now begins to spin an outer, temporary spiral, working towards the edges of the web, and when this is complete it rests for a few minutes. The purpose of this temporary spiral is to stabilize the web during construction and to act as a series of 'stepping-stones' for the spider.

The permanent spiral

When the spider resumes work, the silk issuing from its spinners changes from the dry lines used during the previous ten minutes and now has a sticky coating. The spider retraces its steps along the temporary spiral, this time working its way from the outer edge towards the centre, oil on its feet preventing it from sticking to its own web. As it proceeds it spins a permanent spiral of sticky threads, much more closely set than the temporary one (which is progressively destroyed as the spider advances). This is achieved by holding the thread under its mouth parts and dissolving it with digestive juices. For about twenty minutes the spider painstakingly winds its way towards the centre of the web. Each sticky segment of the new spiral is cemented to a radial line, quickly stretched, then attached to the next radius, while the spider's legs are touching existing lines, enabling it to space the new segments.

Above: Nuctenea umbratica *builds mostly on dead trees and hides its flattened body in a crevice in the bark during the day*

Tidying up

When the spider reaches the gap round the hub it leaves off spinning the viscid spiral, returns to the hub and dissolves the untidy tangle of threads accumulated there. Most spiders immediately replace this with tidy threads but some leave a neat hole in the very centre of the web.

The majority of webs hang in a more or less vertical plane and when the web is complete the spider clings on to the lower side of the hub, settles itself in a comfortable position with its head downwards, draws in its legs and waits for a meal.

Renewal

A successful web is, of course, damaged by the impact and the struggles of the very prey it is designed to catch, and the coating also becomes less sticky in time. Consequently the spider must build a new web every day, using the existing bridge line. The spider consumes the old web first and tests have shown that up to 90% of the silk that is ingested finds its way into the new web so that very little of the spider's substance is wasted. If the web catches no prey, the spider will begin again elsewhere.

INTERACTIONS

*'I think the family is the place where the
most ridiculous and least respectable things
in the world go on'.*

Ugo Betti, *The Inquiry* (1944–5)

So far we have examined many of the curious
behaviour patterns to be found in the spider
world. We have looked at what spiders eat, how
they catch their prey, and how they evade their
enemies. Solitary creatures for the most part,
some of their most interesting behaviour is shown
in their relations with each other.

Curious courtship

The solitary habits and predatory instincts of
spiders can combine to create a serious problem
for the courting male and the males of some
species have evolved ingenious ways to disarm the
females, who might otherwise regard their potential mates as prey. Some male spiders announce
their amorous intentions by plucking gently on the
strands of the female's web, while others opt for
bribery. The *Pisaura mirabilis* male, for instance,
presents a courtship gift of paralysed and silk-
wrapped prey to the female and copulates with her
while she is busy eating her present, whereas the
male of the Eurasian orb-web weaver *Meta*

*Many spiders have developed advanced social
techniques. Here, a male* Pisaura mirabilis *offers a
silk-wrapped insect to his mate*

Above: *when the* Pisaura *male's gift is accepted, the female starts to feed and her attention is distracted from the giver*

(Metellina) segmentata employs a rather less generous courtship technique. He waits at the side of the female's web until an insect blunders into it; as soon as one does so and the female has dashed across to bite and wrap it, he hurries to mate with her while her attention is temporarily distracted by her meal. The wait for an insect to turn up might be a long one, so that in the autumn dozens of anticipatory males can be seen on the outskirts of the web (the female on the hub) their reproductive fortunes hingeing precariously on the arrival of some luckless insect.

With the majority of orb weavers the male stays in the female's web for only an hour or so before taking his leave, but the males of numerous other web-making species spend most of their adult lives with their mates, enjoying, as we have seen, mainly good relations. Over the years I have kept various species of the European House Spider *Tegenaria* and they have rewarded me with some amusing

glimpses into their private lives. *T. gigantea* is, as its name suggests, a formidable-looking spider; the female is up to 18mm in body length, with legs twice as long. One pair I had quickly made themselves at home in an old shoe box containing a cardboard tube for them to hide in during the day. The box was soon filled with sheet web, and flies I tossed in were chased and killed. When there are two spiders after the same prey the nearer one usually gets it, but on one occasion I saw the female rudely push aside her mate and steal the fly he had just caught. I chose to believe that he was chivalrously allowing his egg-laden spouse to feed, but later, while observing another pair, I saw the male chase off the female from her prey and eat it himself — so much for chivalry!

The rarest British *Tegenaria* in houses, *T. parietina*, is a spider of even more imposing dimensions than my other house guests. The legs of the female are up to 50mm long, whilst those of the male can be 80mm. When a friend sent me a pair of these spiders I was delighted, and thinking that such a large species would need a sizeable prey I threw them a grasshopper. Instead of the lusty

chase I had expected, the two spiders went into what I can only describe as a blind panic and headed for the safety of their retreat. Unfortunately they both arrived together and soon became hopelessly entangled, with spindly legs waving in all directions. I was convulsed with laughter and wondered how we humans could possibly fear such timid creatures.

Maternal care

Once spiders have mated and eggs have been laid, the newly-hatched spiderlings can exist for some time on the remains of the yolk, but eventually they must find some tiny prey to catch. In about twenty species, however, the young are provided with food by their mothers. In the case of the European agelenid *Coelotes terrestris*, the spiderlings remain in their mother's web for about a month and during this time she responds to their 'begging' by turning over softened prey to them.

The young of several species of theridiid are fed directly by their mother, chiefly on a regurgitated liquid that they cluster round her mouth to drink. After their first moult, the mother spider catches

Above: the male's cunning strategy having paid off, he promptly seizes his opportunity to mate with the preoccupied female

prey for them and calls the brood down from the retreat by tugging on the web strands. She can easily distinguish between vibrations caused by prey and the movements of her offspring. Even the spiderlings know the difference between calls to eat and alarm vibrations, the latter sending them scurrying to the retreat.

Spider societies

Thirteen species of spider have been found that are truly social, living peacefully in large groups of adults and juveniles and attacking prey co-operatively. In four species of the cribellate *Stegodyphus*, the spiderlings can approach any female in the group to be fed, while an allied species, *Dresserus armatus*, exhibits an even stranger example of social behaviour. The female lays several egg sacs and not only do the first brood scavenge on her remains when she is dead (as a few other spiders do) but they also give food to their more recently

Top: *like theridiid young who feed together, these newly-hatched spiderlings of* Argiope trifasciata *enjoy a communal drink from a raindrop adhering to the strands of silk they have spun*

hatched siblings, feeding their younger brothers and sisters for up to half an hour at a time.

The non-cribellate (ecribellate) species *Agelena republicana* and *Anelosimus eximius*, which weave sheet and tangle webs respectively, co-operate to construct a single giant web, much larger than any solitary spider could make. Hundreds of individuals live on the web and gang up on any large prey that lands on it.

The Paraguayan orb weaver *Eriophora bistriata* bridges the gap between solitary and social behaviour, living in colonies of up to 300 individuals, each building its own web on communally-spun support lines. Small prey is dealt with in the usual way but if it is too large to be tackled by a single spider it attracts the attention of neighbours, who leave their own webs and join in the capture and feeding of the victim.

Some of the *Cyrtophora* species build communal webs but there is no social co-operation here. The juveniles make their smaller webs in the rigging of those of the adult females, but if an unlucky youngster falls into its mother's web it will be seized and eaten! A number of web-building species make individual webs that are very close together but they also do not exhibit any predatory behaviour that can really be described as co-operative. The young common European orb weavers, *Nuctenea cornuta*, for example, sometimes use each other's frame threads, so that numerous webs are packed into a small space.

Intimate relationships

Among the theridiids is a parasitic genus – *Argyrodes* – with numerous species that live on the webs of host spiders and steal their prey: this behaviour is described as *kleptoparasitic*. An even more intimate relationship exists between another spider, *Curimagua bayano*, and its host, the very much larger *Diplura*. The tiny parasite rides, apparently unnoticed, on *Diplura's* body and is able to climb down the chelicerae of its host and share in the 'soup'.

All spiders are predatory, and whilst most of their attention is fixed on insects, all of them indulge in eating their own kind. The habit of cannibalism may be encouraged by the sheer numbers of spiderlings produced from some egg-sacs; the weaker individuals are devoured by their more active siblings.

Most vagrant hunters can run away from each other if they meet but if a hunter falls into a web it is as helpless as any insect. Yet there is one family are *Mimetus* and the smaller *Ero*, both of whom stealthily invade the webs of other species and bite the luckless occupants. *Ero*'s poison is very are *Mimetus* and the smaller *Ero*; the latter stealthily invades the webs of other species and bites the luckless occupants. *Ero*'s poison is very fast-acting on the victim, and in a few seconds the Pirate Spider is feeding on its prey. *E. furcata* can even imitate the courting signals of a male *Meta (Metellina) segmentata* to lure the female.

An unfinished story

The story of the spider is stranger by far than the myth of Arachne, who gave her name to the order

Above: *the 'Pirate Spider'* Ero tuberculata *preys exclusively on other spiders. In this case a young theridiid (right) has fallen victim to the pirate's deadly poison*

of creatures we have been examining. Some 50,000 species from every part of the globe have been identified and described and almost certainly many more species and curious variations in behaviour are still waiting to be discovered. What is beyond doubt, however, is that these adaptable and versatile creatures will continue to exert their fascination on naturalists and laymen alike. We can love spiders or hate them, but once we have had a glimpse into their strange and secret lives we can never wholly ignore them again.

Overleaf: *during the autumn months, the male of the common European spider* Meta (Metellina) segmentata *waits patiently at the edge of the female's web until she approaches a trapped insect. When her energies are concentrated elsewhere, he dashes in to mate with her — a cunning ruse that ensures the survival of the species*

INDEX